ARTHURIAN STUDIES IX

ARTHUR'S KINGDOM OF ADVENTURE

ARTHUR'S KINGDOM OF ADVENTURE

The World of Malory's Morte Darthur

MURIEL WHITAKER

D. S. BREWER · BARNES & NOBLE

Published by D. S. Brewer,
240 Hills Road Cambridge
an imprint of Boydell & Brewer Ltd
PO Box 9, Woodbridge, Suffolk IP12 3DF
and by Barnes and Noble
81 Adams Drive, Totowa, NJ 07512, USA

First published 1984
Reprinted 1986

British Library Cataloguing in Publication Data

Whitaker, Muriel
Arthur's kingdom of adventure: the world of
Malory's Morte darthur.—(Arthurian studies,
ISSN 0261-9814; 10)
1. Malory, *Sir* Thomas. Morte d'Arthur
    I. Title   II. Series
    823′.2   PR2045

ISBN 0-85991-165-9

Library of Congress Cataloging in Publication Data

Whitaker, Muriel A.
Arthur's kingdom of adventure.
(Arthurian studies; 10)
Includes index.
1. Malory, Thomas, Sir, 15th century. Morte d'Arthur.
2. Malory, Thomas, Sir, 15th century—Settings.
3. Arthurian romances—History and criticism.
4. Setting (Literature)
    I. Title.   II. Series.
PR2047.W49 1984   823′.2   84-2773

ISBN 0-389-20474-9

Phototypeset in Great Britain by
Rowland Phototypesetting Ltd, Bury St Edmunds, Suffolk
Printed by St Edmundsbury Press, Bury St Edmunds, Suffolk
and bound by Woolnough Bookbinding,
Wellingborough, Northants

Contents

List of Illustrations

Introduction

The setting of Malory's *Morte Darthur* comprises worlds within worlds, like Chinese ivory balls, each intricately carved and independent yet forming part of a unified structure. At the ideological centre is the castle, symbol of an exclusive aristocratic society; around the castle extends a perilous forest which exists to provide the adventures of knight-errantry. Castles and forests constitute Arthur's realm of England – or Logres, as it is called in its romantic aspect – and this realm, in turn, is enclosed in the empire which Arthur wins by defeating the Roman emperor. Another enclosing orb represents Christendom from the Western islands to the Holy Land where the last of Arthur's knights die fighting against the infidels. Otherworlds – Heaven, Hell, the land of faerie – impinge on the *roiaume aventureux*, their supernatural characters and artefacts sustaining the pervasive moods of wonder and fear.

This Arthurian world which Malory inherited from his sources was artificially constructed to demonstrate concepts of sovereignty, courtesy, knight-errantry and salvation. It exists outside real (historical) time, for in the fifth-century 'Age of Arthur,' Arthur was not the king and in the Age of Chivalry, the king was not Arthur. Yet it is the Age of Chivalry that provides, by means of its images and rituals, the work's continuum. Though only one book, *The Tale of the Sankgreal*, is overtly allegorical, in every book the milieu is composed of images having both literal and figurative meaning. Unless we read these image-studded worlds as Malory's audience did, we fail to understand Malory's *Morte Darthur* in the fullest sense.

TO THE MEMORY OF
LUCIE POLAK

1

The Sword and the Crown

Whether the original Arthur was a god, a culture hero, or a *dux bellorum* of the Brythonic Celts who fought against the Saxons in the late fifth century,[1] the Arthur of Malory's *Morte Darthur* is a romantic hero in a historical or pseudo-historical context. When Geoffrey of Monmouth first presented Arthur as a medieval monarch and a continental conqueror,[2] it is possible that his concept of the British king may have been influenced by the figure of Charlemagne[3] in French history and legend. It may also have been influenced by the character and achievements of William the Conqueror.[4] The author of Malory's English source, the alliterative *Morte Arthure*, may have taken as a model Edward III,[5] and Malory himself may have idealized in Arthur the prestigious Henry V[6] or his own immediate overlord, Richard Beauchamp, Earl of Warwick, under whom the Warwickshire knight served at the siege of Calais.[7] Historical analogies[8] may well account for the realism which sometimes characterizes Malory's treatment of the chronicle material. Nevertheless, romantic elements are sufficiently important for Arthur to be regarded as a romantic hero whose biography reflects that 'close union of the primeval and magical with hard-headed politics' which for Friedrich Heer constituted the atmosphere of courtly romance.[9]

The traditional hero pattern of royal ancestry, mysterious conception and birth, protected childhood, magical recognition, preliminary successes, crucial struggle, victory, and apotheosis is well illustrated in the traditional life of Arthur. It is these aspects of the biography that may be regarded as mythic.[10] Through his father, King Uther Pendragon, he is linked to the legendary kings of Britain, descendants of the Trojan prince, Brutus.[11] Through his mother, Igraine, he is related to the Celtic enchantress, Morgan le Fay. His illicit conception is contrived by Merlin, the magician who brings Uther to Igraine in the guise of her husband. Spirited away at birth for his own protection, the child is brought up secretly. His right to the throne is proved at the appointed time by the magical test of the sword in the stone. His victories over the rebellious kings are effected with the assistance of Merlin and through the potency of his own magical weapons. In a crucial struggle he kills first the giant of St Michael's Mount, then the Roman Emperor. He marries a princess, Guenevere, and receives a marvellous wedding present, the Round Table. Finally, after a fatal battle, he is transported to the Celtic Otherworld, Avalon,[12] to be healed of his wounds. From there he will return to save his people.[13] This is the mythic core of the medieval Arthur.

In the centuries preceding Malory's, the character of Arthur had been subject to a variety of representations. The Arthur of Celtic myth had been a tribal hero who led his band of warriors on Otherworld quests and monster-slaying adventures as in *Kulhwch and Olwen* or *The Spoils of Annwfn*. The Arthur of the Latin *Vitae* was a local tyrant with, in E. K. Chambers' apt phrase, 'an undisciplined character which occasionally calls for saintly correction'.[14] In the French romances he was a *roi fainéant*, a 'banal maître de ceremonies'.[15] The *Perlesvaus* depicted him as a ruler whose sloth had undermined the Round Table and enervated the whole kingdom while in Robert de Boron's *Mort d'Arthur* his continental expedition was only a minor adventure undertaken to help Lancelot regain his lands from a usurper. In the *Prose Lancelot* he was so weak that he could not protect his vassal Ban nor avenge his death[16] and he was powerless to prevent the theft of his golden cup in *Li Contes del Graal* or the abduction of his queen in *Le Chevalier de la Charrette*. None of these versions of the Arthurian material except the Welsh treats Arthur as a hero.

Therefore, Malory turned to the English chronicle tradition which depicted Arthur as a great British king, continental conqueror, and Christian champion. For Malory and most of his contemporaries Arthur was a historical personage. Attempts to discredit his historicity were rigorously resisted for hundreds of years after the appearance of Geoffrey's *Historia*. The fourteenth-century *Scalacronica* of Sir Thomas Gray includes 'a hole Chapitre speking agayne them that beleve not Arthure to have beene King of Britaine'.[17] Caxton, too, firmly condemns those who deny[18] that there 'was suche a noble kyng named Arthur, and reputed one of the nine worthy, and fyrst and chyef of the Cristen men'. As proof of Arthur's historicity he offers not only the numerous chronicles, but his tomb at Glastonbury,[19] his seal in Westminster Abbey, Gawain's skull[20] and Cradoc's mantle in Dover Castle, the Round Table[21] at Winchester, Lancelot's sword and many other things 'in other places'.[22] Finally, as an indication that Malory himself probably accepted the historicity of Arthur there is his colophon at the conclusion of the Roman Wars episode:

Here endyth the Tale of the Noble Kynge Arthure that was Emperoure hymself thorow dygnyté of his hondys.

(247)

10

Medieval visions of history synthesized three pasts – the Judeo-Christian, the Graeco-Roman and the national barbarian.[23] The life of a national hero was part of the linear progress of world history rather than an isolated and merely personal phenomenon. Through the use of genealogy, Malory relates the biography of Arthur to the frame of world history as devised by Christian historiographers. Arthur's father, Uther Pendragon, is a pseudo-historical son of the historical Constantine the Great who proclaimed himself Roman Emperor at York in 306 AD, removed the seat of empire to the shores of the Bosphorus and accepted the Christian faith, earning for himself in the words of Gibbon, 'every attribute of a hero, and even of a saint'. Malory's Arthur cites this ancestry, as well as his relationship to an earlier pair of British conquerors, Belyn and Bryne, in order to establish his right to undertake the quest for Rome. The message which the senators deliver to the Roman Emperor Lucius asserts Arthur's belief that

Ye have ocupyed the Empyre with grete wronge, for all his [i.e. Arthur's] trew auncettryes sauff his fadir Uther were Emperoures of Rome.

(192)

Furthermore, Malory's description (not in his source) of Constantine as 'dame Elyneys son' and the allusion to the recovery of the True Cross produce the synthesis of national, classical and Christian 'history' that the figure of Constantine represented in the Middle Ages. Arthur, the descendant of Constantine, belongs clearly to the tradition of 'Christianissimus rex', an idealized type created by such medieval historiographers as Asser, Suger, and Bede.

While the family tree is important in establishing the hero's credentials, the idea of kingship in medieval iconography is commonly conveyed by such images as the crown, the sword, the sceptre, the orb, and the throne. The medieval artist made little distinction between the biblical, the historical and the romantic; Saul, David, and Solomon, Charlemagne and Edward IV, Brutus and Arthur are similarly depicted, enthroned and crowned, holding an upright sword, usually in the left hand. Three gold crowns on shield, surcoat, or pennon is the heraldic device that identifies Arthur among the Nine Worthies on such diverse artefacts as the tapestries (c. 1400) in the Cloisters Museum, New York; the murals of the Castle of La Manta in Piedmont; the stained glass windows in the Rathaus of Lüneberg, Germany; and the mortuary chest of Robert Curthose in Gloucester Cathedral.[24] The images of crown and sword are particularly relevant to the romance of Arthur whose genealogy entitled him to the crown but whose right had to be demonstrated publicly by success in the sword test. Malory's description of the artefact is unusually explicit:

. . . there was sene in the chircheyard ayenst the hyhe aulter a grete stone four square, lyke unto a marbel stone, and in myddes therof was lyke an anvylde of stele a foot on hyghe, and theryn stack a fayre swerd naked by the poynt, and letters there were wryten in gold about the swerd that saiden thus: 'WHOSO PULLETH OUTE THIS SWERD OF THIS STONE AND ANVYLD IS RIGHTWYS KYNGE BORNE OF ALL ENGLOND.'

(12)

According to J. R. Reinhard,[25] the sword and stone have a *geasa* laid on them so that they will only yield to the hero destined to succeed.

In the *Morte Darthur* the test is devised by an unlikely pair of collaborators – Merlin, the son of a nun and a devil, and the Archbishop of Canterbury – so that a Christian context is provided for what must originally have been a gift from the pagan Otherworld. Later on, when this first Excalibur fails the king in an encounter with King Pellinore, it is replaced by a less equivocal weapon and this time the Archbishop of Canterbury is not involved:

And as they rode, kynge Arthur seyde, 'I have no swerde.' 'No force,' seyde Merlyon, 'hereby ys a swerde that shall be youre, and I may.'
So they rode tyll they com to a laake that was a fayre watir and brode. And in the myddis Arthure was ware of an arme clothed in whyghte samyte, that helde a fayre swerde in that honde.

(52)

Following Merlin's directions, Arthur speaks courteously to the Lady of the Lake who has reached them by walking across the water from her great palace in the rock. In exchange for the promise of a gift to be paid on demand, Arthur acquires the sword, also called Excalibur, by taking it from the hand in the lake.

Excalibur's existence in the natural world coincides almost exactly with the temporal extent of Arthur's reign for its acquisition marks the beginning of his sovereignty and its relinquishment the end. As well as being a sign of kingship, it functions, through its scabbard, as a protective amulet. Merlin explains that

'. . . the scawberde ys worth ten of the swerde; for whyles ye have the scawberde uppon you ye shall lose no blood, be ye never so sore wounded. Therefore kepe well the scawberde allweyes with you'.

(54)

Because the sword and scabbard together represent Arthur's sovereign power, longevity, and invulnerability, associations of treachery accrue to them through the machinations of the malicious Morgan le Fay. After a second warning from Merlin, the king entrusts the scabbard to his half-sister, who passes it to her lover Accolon and substitutes a similar looking scabbard and sword that she has made through magic. Deprived of his talisman and his own good sword, Arthur almost bleeds to death in a subsequent battle with Accolon until the Damosel of the Lake intervenes, so that 'by the damesels inchauntemente the swerde Excaliber fell oute of Accolon's honde to the erthe, and there withall Sir Arthure lyghtly lepe to hit and gate hit in his honde, and forthwithall he knew hit that hit was his swerde Excalyber' (144). The scabbard, however, is soon lost forever. Pursued by her brother after the revelation of her treachery, Morgan

> rode unto a lake thereby and seyde, 'Whatsoever com of me, me brothir shall nat have this scawberde!' And than she lete throwe the scawberde in the deppyst of the watir. So hit sanke, for hit was hevy of golde and precious stonys.
>
> (151)

The incident foreshadows the dual disloyalties of the king's other close female relative, Guenevere, and of Bedevere whose reluctance to dispose of the sword contrasts with Morgan's expedition in jettisoning the scabbard. It also makes inevitable the mortal wound inflicted by Mordred on the Day of Destiny.

The iconography of the sword includes other associations relevant to Arthur, those of chivalry, conquest, and justice. Success in the sword test is insufficient proof of sovereign right in the eyes of the many angry lords who 'saide it was grete shame unto them all and the reame to be overgovernyd with a boye of no hyghe blood borne'. After Arthur has repeatedly demonstrated his ability to draw the sword from the stone at Candlemas, Easter, and Pentecost, it is the common people who cry out:

> 'We wille have Arthur unto our kyng! . . . for we all see that it is Goddes wille.'
>
> (16; Malory's addition)

Then the young hero takes Excalibur between his hands and offers it on the altar in the presence of the Archbishop of Canterbury[26] who makes him a knight before crowning him king. The final stage in the assumption of sovereignty is the king's oath 'to stand with true justyce fro thens forth the dayes of this lyf'. As Vinaver points out,[27] Malory's association of sovereignty with the support of the commons and with the administration of justice is not derived from his French sources. Furthermore, the idea that the king is first of all a knight, that the sword takes precedence over the crown, is a Malorian concept that makes it possible for Arthur to enjoy the adventures of a knight-errant. But the most important statement of associated values occurs much later, when Sir Mador, refusing to withdraw his charge of treason against the queen, demands that Arthur grant him the right to participate in a *duel judiciaire*

> for thoughe ye be oure kynge, in that degré ye ar but a knyght as we ar, and ye ar sworne unto knyghthode als welle as we be.
>
> (1050; Malory's addition)

To establish the kingdom the young ruler must wield his sword against the dissidents. Excalibur flashes so brightly that like the weapon of a sun god it blinds the eyes of the enemy. In subjugating the rebels, Arthur takes on the qualities of an epic hero, whose *topos*, as described by E. R. Curtius,[28] includes battle-lore, manliness in the field and in the war council, and proficiency in the use of a particular weapon. Merlin provides 'the wisdom of experience in the man of great age' to assist the hero in devising a strategy that will unify his kingdom. In a continuation of the hero pattern, he marries a wife and establishes a fellowship of knights. But he cannot achieve his full stature until he has carried the sword abroad and brought the crown imperial to Britain.

Since Rome was the world empire best known to medieval historiographers, its crown symbolized unequaled power and glory in the temporal sphere. Far from being an example of 'unfortunate imperialism' as it was in Geoffrey's *Historia*,[29] or an occasion for proud self-indulgence, as it becomes in the alliterative *Morte Arthure*,[30] the journey to Rome is the most glorious event in Malory's biography of Arthur. Not only does it prove Arthur's power and worthiness as national hero but it further develops Malory's concepts of chivalry and sovereignty. It is an idealisation of history embodying the dream of continental supremacy which English claims to French lands had fostered since the Norman Conquest.

When *The Tale of the Noble King Arthur* begins, more than twenty years have passed since the youthful hero had drawn the sword from the stone. Lancelot, whom Merlin had seen as an infant in the land of Benwick, has now grown up and come to court. Arthur has fulfilled the destiny proclaimed by Merlin at the coronation feast:

> . . . he shal be kyng and overcome alle his enemyes, and or he deye he shalle be long kynge of all Englond and have under his obeyssaunce Walys, Yrland, and Scotland, and moo reames than I will now reherce.
>
> (18; Malory's addition)

His territories have been extended to the continent by the acquisition of 'many fayre contrayes that Arthure had wonne before of the myghty kynge Claudas' (194; Malory's addition). The Round Table has been established as Arthur's administrative arm, settling disputes, righting wrongs and maintaining peace throughout the kingdom. Merlin, the architect of Arthur's early successes, has long been imprisoned under 'the grete stone'. The structure of *Morte Darthur* now demands a climactic victory before the history of Arthur is interrupted by the cyclic adventures of knight-errantry. The story of Arthur's Roman Wars which Malory found in the alliterative *Morte Arthure* provides the means of testing the king's heroic qualities and demonstrating the ideals which he embodies.

The historical quest is initiated by a romantic convention. As Arthur is presiding over 'a ryal feeste and Table Rounde', the ceremonies are interrupted by the arrival of strangers who present a challenge that cannot be ignored:

'. . . the gretis welle Lucius, the Emperour of Roome, and commaundis the uppon payne that woll falle to sende hym the trewage of this realme that thy fadir Uther Pendragon payde, other ellys he woll bereve the all thy realmys that thou weldyst, and thou as rebelle, not knowynge hym as thy soverayne, withholdest and reteynest, contrary to the statutes and decrees maade by the noble and worthy Julius Cezar, conquerour of this realme'.

(186; the allusions to Uther and Caesar are Malory's addition)

In the world of chivalric romance, a challenge results in the immediate departure from court of a single knight of the Round Table or a small group of knights. A different ritual is followed in the historical quest. Though Arthur himself controls the action and is the chief participant, he must have the approbation and military support of all those who owe him feudal allegiance.[31] He calls a council of noble lords and 'the moste party of the knyghtes of the Rounde Table' (187; Malory's addition). 'The Conqueror', as he is designated in this tale, is supported by lords of England, Cornwall, Little Britain, West Wales, Ireland, Argyle, the Outer Isles and France. Though Arthur had defeated the King of Denmark in the War with the Five Kings and presumably had gained the allegiance of Scandinavia, the Northern allies mentioned by Geoffrey (HRB IX, XIX) and the alliterative poet (11. 44–47) are omitted by Malory, no doubt because he wanted the glory of the achievement to fall entirely on Arthur and 'oure noble knyghtes of mery Ingelonde' (209; Malory's addition).

In the organization of the imperial quest, two further aspects of Malory's originality should be noted. The aggrandizement of Lancelot which occurs throughout the Roman Wars[32] is initiated at the council of war where he is presented as an ardent young knight and as a substantial feudal lord of France. While Lancelot's role is increased, that of Mordred is omitted. The king's nephew – or son – had traditionally fulfilled the function of regent during Arthur's absence,[33] but Malory's Arthur appoints as co-regents Sir Baudwen of Britagne and Sir Constantine, Arthur's designated heir. Vinaver sees the historical analogy of Henry V's appointment of Bishop Beaufort and the Duke of Bedford as the source of Malory's change[34] but it is just as likely that the concept of the historical quest as an event that demonstrated Arthur's invincibility and earthly glory precluded the mention of his nemesis.

The romantic quests of the knight-errant occur in a vaguely defined world of castles and perilous forests while the spiritual quests of the Grail knights take place in allegorical landscapes that reflect the moral and spiritual condition of man. In contrast, the historical quest follows a clearly marked route that had long been familiar to legionaries, crusaders, merchants and pilgrims[35] and that is now followed by the envoys of the Roman Emperor, hurrying out of England at Arthur's command:

> Thus they passed fro Carleyle unto Sandwyche-warde . . . and by the sonne was sette at the seven dayes ende they come unto Sandwyche . . . And so the same nyght they toke the watir and passed into Flaundres, Almayn, and aftir that over the grete mountayne that hyght Godarde, and so aftir thorow Lumbardy and thorow Tuskayne, and sone aftir they come to the Emperour Lucius.
>
> (191)

It is the same route that Arthur will take. Barfleet, Paris, Soissons, Cologne, Lucerne, Milan, Pontremoli, Spoleto, Viterbo, and the virtuous vale of Vysecounte with 'vynys full' are stages of the progress to 'the cité of Syon that is Rome callyd' (244) where Arthur intends to hold a Round Table as evidence of the quest's successful completion.

It is the nature of a quest to invite interruption. The final goal cannot be reached until the hero's prowess has been proven in combat and his power of restoring order demonstrated. The idea of the quest as a redemptive process is reflected in Arthur's encounters with the giant of St Michael's Mount and with the Emperor Lucius, both sources of evil in the environment. By his victories the hero not only demonstrates his superiority but also effects that improvement of society which is the hero's true function.

As Arthur passes over the water from the known world of Britain to the unknown world of the continent, an allegorical dream prepares him for the fearful struggles that lie ahead.[36] The hero's acquisition of knowledge through warning and prophecy is a conventional technique of the romance author, enabling him to create an atmosphere of foreboding while, at the same time, establishing faith in the hero's prowess and ultimate success. It is probable that the magnificent dragon symbolizing Arthur in the dream vision is ultimately derived from the dragon ensign of the Romans, an image that denoted the cohort and that, coloured red or purple, was used by the emperor for ceremonial as well as bellicose occasions.[37] Arthur inherited the dragon sign from his father, Uther Pendragon, whose title was suggested by the victorious red dragon under Vortigern's tower and by the dragon-shaped star that

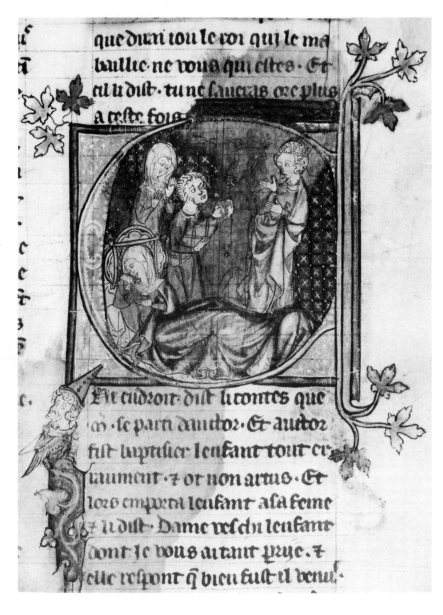

que dixai tou le roi qui le me
baillie ne vous qui estes · Et
til li dist · tu ne sauctas oxe plus
a teste fois

Et endroit · dist li contes que
as · se part auctor · Et auctor
fist baptisier lenfant tout er
taument · 7 or non artus · Et
lors emporta lenfant asa feme
7 li dist · Dame vesch lenfant
dont le vous ai tant prye · 7
elle respont q bien fust il venus

1. After Igraine has given birth to Arthur, Merlin takes the baby. Huth Merlin
(London, British Library, Add. MS.38117 f.66)

foretold his defeat of the Saxons.[38] By the thirteenth century, the dragon was so firmly established as a military device associated with Arthur that the illustrators of an Old French *Merlin* (ca. 1290) showed a cloth dragon with vermilion wings and a green head flying from the top of a staff at the forefront of battle.[39]

In 1244, according to the Chronicle of Ralph of Coggeshall, Henry III ordered Edward, his goldsmith, painter and vestment-maker, to create as an ensign a dragon of red samite and gold, with a moveable tongue like fire and eyes made of sapphires or other precious stones. The standard was to be placed in Westminster Abbey.[40] One wonders if some such jewelled replica might have inspired the author of the alliterative *Morte*:

Bothe his hede and hys hals ware halely all over
Oundyde of azure, enamelde[41] full faire;
His schoulders ware schalyde all in clene sylvere,
Schreede over all the schrympe with schrinkande poyntez;
In meruaylous maylys he mountede full hye; . . .
And syche a vennymous flayre flowe fro his lyppez,
That the flode of the flawez all on fyre semyde

(11. 764–773)

The head of Malory's dragon is 'enamyled with asure', his shoulders shine with gold, his stomach is like mail of marvellous colour and his claws are 'lyke clene golde'. This combination of coloured glass and bright metal produces the effect of light that was an expression of the divine and the ideal.[42] Far from being a representation of evil, this dragon, as a philosopher tells the king, nobly represents

thyne owne persone that thus here sayles with thy syker knyghtes; and the coloure of his wyngys is thy kyngdomes that thou haste with thy knyghtes wonne. And his tayle that was all to-tatered sygnyfyed your noble knyghtes of the Rounde Table.

(197)

In contrast, the horrible bear that represents 'som tyraunte that turmentis thy peple' or 'som gyaunt' is presented in demonic imagery – 'all blak, in a clowde', 'his pawys were as byg as a poste', 'all to-rongeled with lugerande lokys', 'the fowlyst beste that ever ony man sye'. Its 'grysly tuskes' tear the dragon's flesh so violently that the sea becomes blood red. The bear image foreshadows the repugnant giant of St Michael's Mount and the demonic setting in which he is found.

The episode of Arthur's fight with the giant 'goes back to very remote mythical antiquity'.[43] Malory adopts the expanded version of the story which he found in the alliterative *Morte Arthure* and gives it a moral significance that Geoffrey's account lacked.[44] No sooner has Arthur landed in Normandy than he is told that a great giant, an oppressor of Arthur's subjects for more than seven years, has just kidnapped the Duchess of Brittany. As heroic king and conqueror, it is Arthur's duty to eradicate the evil. Adopting the metaphor of a pilgrimage, that is, of a religious quest, Arthur sets out with Bedevere and Kay in search of 'the saint'. From a 'blythe contray full of many myrry byrdis' Arthur climbs alone to the crest of the crag with its cold wind, flaming fires, wailing widow, new marked grave, captive maidens, spitted children and gnawed bones. This is 'the world that desire totally rejects: the world of the nightmare and the scapegoat, of bondage and pain and confusion'.[45]

The demonic nature of the giant and the heroic quality of Arthur are conveyed not only by means of the landscape associated with each but also by their appearance. Arthur in his jesserant, bascinet, and broad shield is 'clenly arayed'. His sovereignty is signified by his crown, his chivalry by his sword, and his Christianity by his dagger, a symbol of trust in God. The giant, in contrast, is a satanic figure illustrating Rosemond Tuve's perception that 'allegorical elements enter the imagery in the form farthest removed from ordinary realism and closest to "realized idea"'.[46] His physical ugliness reflects his evil disposition. Animal images denote his bestiality. Like the bear in Arthur's dream, he is 'the fowlyste freyke that ever was fourmed' and 'the foulyst wyghte that ever man sye'; 'there was never devil in helle more horryblyer made'. He is a 'doggys son' with teeth like a greyhound. He gnaws on the limb of a man and the flesh of Christian children. He is a murderer, a rapist, a cannibal. Instead of a sword he carries an iron club, the characteristic weapon of giants and a symbol of brutality and social inferiority. He fights according to no rules, relying on his physical strength to crush his victim. In addition to his physical appearance and bestial habits, fire imagery evokes a demonic association. On the top of the crag Arthur finds 'two fyres flamand full hyghe'. Beside one is the new grave of the Duchess; by the other the breechless giant warms himself while his macabre meal is prepared – 'twelve chyldir but late borne, and they were broched in maner lyke birdes'.

The emphasis on physical dismemberment reinforces still further the demonic atmosphere. The giant's genitals are 'swapped in sunder', his forehead cloven to the brain, and his belly cut 'that oute went the gore, that the grasse and the grounde all foule was begone'. The giant defiles the scene in much the same way as do the devils in the milieu of the Grail quest.

The extensiveness of treatment here in comparison with the cursory giant killing episodes associated with Lancelot in later adventures suggests that, like the author of the alliterative *Morte Arthure*,[47] Malory attached moral implications to the old hero tale, a view supported by the ending. The king's victory is marked by the public exhibition of the giant's head, the distribution of treasure to the knights (Malory's addition), and the building of a church on the mountain to signify the triumph of good over evil, rather than to commemorate the murdered Duchess.[48] In this way the primitive concept of the culture hero ridding the land of monsters in order to benefit mankind is assimilated into the medieval view of the sovereign's responsibility for the maintenance of law and order.

The bear 'oute of the Oryent' in Arthur's dream signifies not only the folkloric opponent but also the 'historical' foe. The rivalry between the Eastern Empire of Byzantium and a Western Europe partitioned into barbarian successor states determines the composition of the opposing forces in Arthur's continental war. The Roman Emperor summons allies from the reaches of the Graeco-Roman world (the influence of the Alexander legends and of the Crusades may be seen here)[49] – Alexandria, India, Armenia, Assyria, Africa, 'Europe the large', the Outer Isles, Arabia, Damascus, Egypt, Damietta, Cappadocia, Tarsus, Turkey, Persia, Pamphylia, Syria, the land of Prester John, from Nero to Nazareth, from Greece to Galilee, Cyprus, Macedonia, Calabria, Catalonia, Portugal and Spain. Malory's addition of the last two countries to the traditional catalogue indicates that by the fifteenth century the geographic focus had shifted to the west as a result, perhaps, of Portuguese voyages of discovery and the Spanish expulsion of the Moors. Just as the giant of St Michael's Mount greatly surpassed Arthur in size, so the number of resources of Lucius' army, consisting not only of kings and dukes with their 'horryble peple' but also of fifty giants, engendered by fiends, far outweighs Arthur's forces. It is a romantic convention that seemingly insuperable barriers should impede the progress of the quest. Yet a Roman senator is forced to admit what every reader of romance knows, 'For this day one of Arthur's knyghtes was worth in batayle an hondred of oures' (218; Malory's addition).

The demonic nature of Lucius' army is revealed by its composition – which includes demon-bred giants and Saracens – and by its actions. At the council of state preceding the quest, King Angwysh reminds Arthur:

> And Scotlonde had never scathe syne ye were crowned kynge, and whan the Romaynes raynede uppon us they raunsomed oure elders and raffte us of our lyves.
>
> (188)

Now, as Lucius makes his way westward, fair countries are destroyed, conquered castles in Christian lands are manned by pagans, innocent people are murdered. 'Where that he rydyth all he destroyes' the marshal of France reports and Lucius himself announces, 'for the douchery of Britayne I shall thorowly dystroy hit'.

Arthur is equally implacable in his determination to wipe out the enemy. No gold under God will save their lives. It is better that the Emperor and his lords sink into hell than that a Round Table knight be wounded. Those that 'accompany them with Sarezens' do not deserve to live (Malory's addition). The religious allusions are consistent with the depiction of Arthur as a Christian Champion.

The use of animal images derived from the rhetorical storehouse of Anglo-Saxon battle poems contributes to the contrast between the Britons and Romans. In 'the thycheste of the pres' Arthur 'raumped doune lyke a lyon many senatours noble'. Sir Bors and Sir Berrell, not to be outdone, fight like two boars. In contrast, Priam's Saracens follow him 'as shepe oute of a folde', so willing are they to desert the Romans and join Arthur. When Sir Kay is wounded, Cliges and Bedivere 'fared with the Romaynes as grayhoundis doth with harys'. In each case it is Arthur and his knights who exhibit the nobility, strength and skill of the lion, boar, and hound while the enemy is equated with the weaker and more timid animals.

While Lucius and his forces symbolize evil, they also embody the power and glory that Arthur claims.[50] Rich imagery is used to evoke the Roman *imperium*. The envoys sent by Lucius to Arthur's court are 'xij ancyen men berynge eche of them a braunche of Olyve in token that they cam as Embassatours';[51] in token, too, of the *pax Romana* that St Augustine had praised. When the Arthurian knights approach the Roman camp for the first time they see

> many prowde pavylyons of sylke of dyverse coloures that were sette in a medow besyde a ryver, and the Emperoures pavylyon was in the myddys with an egle displayed on loffte.
>
> (206)

Sir Bors is opposed by 'a gay knight . . . all floryshed in golde' and by 'a bolde barowne all in purpull arayed' (208). Sir Priam is splendid in a hauberk of mail studded with rubies. The symbolic eagle and the imperial colours on the battlefield create the aura of Roman magnificence to which Arthur later pays tribute in the funerary arrangements for the dead Emperor, his allies and senators:

> The kynge let bawme all thes with many good gummys and setthen lette lappe hem in syxtyfolde of sendell large, and than lete lappe hem in lede that for chauffynge other chongyng they sholde never savoure, and sytthen lete close them in chestys full clenly arayed, and their baners abovyn on their bodyes, and their shyldys turned upwarde, that eviry man myght knowe of what contray they were.
>
> (225)

When the Roman Ambassadors had reported back to Lucius after their hasty retreat from Arthur's court, they had described the British monarch as 'the royallyst kynge that lyvyth on earthe' and the knights of the Round Table

20

as nonpareils; 'of wysedome and of fayre speeche and all royalté and rychesse they fayle of none'. Malory omits the lengthy description of the Christmas Day feast which in the alliterative *Morte Arthure* suggests the brilliance and sophistication of the English court. Instead, he relies on the imagery of the battlefield to convey the chivalric stature of Arthur and his knights: Lancelot's banners, Gawain's 'bowerly bronde that bryght semed', Arthur's 'clene' arms with their 'doleful dragon', Uwayne's bright sword that strikes down the Emperor's standard, Excalibur cutting the giant Galapas 'of by the kneis clenly', and finally cleaving the Emperor 'frome the creste of his helme unto the bare pappys'.

The hyperbole that characterizes romance is apparent in the description of the battle. Kay, Clegis, and Bedevere in one encounter kill more than five hundred. Sir Lancelot and his friends slay so many that 'thousandis in an hepe lay thrumbelyng togedir'. Arthur himself, 'raumping doune lyke a lyon' kills a hundred thousand – 'Was never kyng nother knyghtes dud bettir syn God made the worlde.'

The glorification of Arthur is moral as well as political and military. There is a conflict not only of nations but of ideas and ideals, of Christianity against paganism, good rule against bad, justice and mercy against brutality and arrogance, the chivalric conduct of the few Arthurian knights against the ruthless force of the enemy hordes. There is no confusion regarding the identity of friends and foe, no disparity between appearance and reality, as there so often is in the world of knight-errantry. The enemy is rigorously suppressed; only the joust between Gawain and Priamus ends in the romantic way, with the conversion of the enemy and his absorption into the Round Table.

Many of Malory's original additions are designed to elucidate the contrasts between the forces of good and the forces of evil both by expressions of authorial opinion and by the use of appropriate images. When the army of Lucius invades France, destroying the country and slaughtering the people, Arthur sends the Emperor a message:

> '. . . sey I bydde hym in haste to remeve oute of my londys. And yf he woll nat, so bydde hym dresse his batayle and lette us redresse oure ryghtes with oure handis, and that is more worshyppe than thus to overryde maysterlesse men'.
>
> (206)

On the battlefield a man should be governed by his virtues, not his vices. Excessive hardiness is foolish 'whan knyghtes bene overmacched'. A desire for fame should not overcome one's feelings of humanity:

21

for oftetymes thorow envy grete hardynesse is shewed that hath bene the
deth of many kyd knyghtes; for thoughe they speke fayre many one unto
other, yet whan they be in batayle eyther wolde beste be praysed.

(223)

A desire for gold and silver should not persuade one to spare God's enemies;
'the man that wolde save them were lytyll to prayse' (224). While adding
passages which reveal his idea of a good knight, Malory omits episodes in his
source which detract from the ideality of Arthur and his Round Table. The
insults which Gawain hurls at Lucius, Arthur's violent rages, the ravaging of
the countryside by the knights, the taking of children as hostages, the motive of
revenge, and the harsh treatment of the vanquished are among the omissions
which enable Malory to maintain the ideality of the quest.

Furthermore, idealisation characterizes the quest's milieu. Isolated images
rather than the lengthy rhetorical descriptions of the source are the means of
depicting the battlefields, unchanging throughout the episodic combats that
interrupt the progress to Rome. Trumpets and tabours, severed heads, spilling
guts, swords stained with gore and brains, corpses lying on the bare earth,
swords striking sparks from helmets, and coursers charging across the field,
trampling the fallen underfoot – these images evoke the violence and excite-
ment of the scene. As in medieval tapestries and illuminations, the foreground
is crowded with armed men, horses, swords, shields, and standards. The
dragon image appears twice. At the Battle of Sessoyne the Roman Emperor
raises an ensign – 'a dragon with eglys many one enewed with sabyl'[52] and the
Welsh king's arms are emblazoned with a 'dolefull dragon'. The thin vermilion
streaks that represent blood in the miniatures are paralleled by references to
'the raylyng bloode' that falls down to the Emperor's feet, Gawain's armour 'all
blody berenne', and the brain and blood on the sword Galantine.

Mêlées alternate with single combats, the paired warriors occupying the
foreground while bowmen, knights, giants, coursers engage in 'a stronge
batayle on every syde' (220). These engagements are the historical counterparts of the jousts and tournaments which fill the romantic milieu.

An important aspect of Malory's originality in *The Tale of King Arthur and
the Emperor Lucius* is the structural change effected by his long postponement
of the denouement. In other chronicles of Arthur, the king is recalled to
England by Mordred's rebellion before Rome has been reached. A speedy
reversal of fortune follows the king's continental successes, depriving him of
queen, kingdom, knights and life. Arthur's downfall is attributed to *hubris*, the
waging of unjust wars, and the turn of Fortune's wheel.

From a structural point of view, the Emperor's death, which occurs in the
vale of Soissons in May, leaves Malory with a large distance, spatially and
temporally, to be covered before Arthur can be crowned in Rome at Christmas.
For the author of the *Morte Arthure*, the death of Lucius is a pivotal point

marking Arthur's turning from a just war against pagans and Roman oppressors to wars of aggression against Christian nations. The philosopher who interprets Arthur's dream of Fortune condemns his violence:

> Thow has schedde myche blode and schalkes distroyede,
> Sakeles in cirquytrie in sere kynges landis . . .
> I rede thow rekkyn and reherse unresonable dedis,
> Or the repenttes full rathe all thi rewthe werkes.
>
> (11. 3398–9; 3452–3)

Arthur's treatment of conquered peoples and his unbridled ambition are the cause of his downfall.

Malory, however, must present subsequent events in such a way that they will not denigrate the hero or weaken the Round Table. The action must move towards the climactic coronation in Rome, attended by all the great knights. Kay and Bedevere, who had been killed by the Romans in the *Morte Arthure*, are therefore preserved in Malory's version and the warlike activities of the knights are presented as exercises in self-defence. In a passage without parallel in the source Priam warns:

> 'ye shall fynde in yondir woodys many perellus knyghtes. They woll putte furth beystys to bayte you oute of numbir, and ye ar fraykis in this fryth nat paste seven hondred, and that is feythfully to fewe to fyght with so many, for harlottys and haynxmen wol helpe us but a lytyll, for they woll hyde them in haste for all their hyghe wordys'.
>
> (235)

The imbalance of the forces in favour of the enemy justifies the Arthurian knights' engagement in combat.

The atmosphere of romance is evoked by the treatment of the Gawain-Priamus adventure with its ritual of challenge and response, the *courtoisie* of the combatants, the ideal spring landscape, and the marvelous healing waters of Paradise that cure the terrible wounds. The king's anger at the defiance of the Tuscan city is balanced by his graciousness to the suppliant ladies who 'kneled downe unto the kynge and besought hym of his grace' (242; not in the source).

Many violent war scenes are greatly reduced or omitted altogether. In *Morte Arthure* the ravaging of Tuscany is described in detail:

> Thus thy spryngene and sprede, and sparis but lyttille,
> Spoylles dispetouslye and spillis theire vynes;
> Spendis un-sparely, that sparede was longe,
> Spedis theme to Spolett with speris inewe!
>
> (11. 3158–3161)

Malory portrays Tuscany as an idyllic setting where Arthur sojourns 'with solace at his harte' in a 'vertuouse vale amonge vynys full'. The effect of imagery in conveying atmosphere is illustrated by the contrast between the trampled vineyards of the first description and the flourishing vines of the second.

By treating the continental expedition not as epic or tragedy but as chivalric quest, Malory can conduct Arthur to Rome and allow him to return to the acclamation of his court in London, utilizing the same structural pattern of withdrawl and return that characterizes the adventures in the romantic and religious milieux. Although he may have read the description of Arthur's coronation in John Harding's *Chronicle*[54] (ca. 1435), the only chronicle in which Arthur reaches Rome, it is not unreasonable to suppose that Malory himself devised the Roman ceremony as a fitting conclusion to the wars and one which demonstrated Arthur's superiority as knight and Christian king. He had been preceded to Rome by the legates, who had announced his imperial designs, and by the tribute of corpses, 'the tane and the trewage of ten score wynters bothe of Ingelonde, Irelonde, and of all the Est londys'. He had demonstrated on the road to Rome his worthiness to hold imperial power. The giant of St Michael's Mount had been overcome, the Romans and their pagan allies defeated, the ladies of Tuscany protected, the king's valour, justice, mercy, moderation, and affection for his knights demonstrated. The conquered had promised to 'make homage unto Arthure all his lyff tymes'. Church and State in the persons of cardinals and senators had besought him 'to be crowned in Rome 'kyndly, with crysemed hondys, with septure, forsothe, as an Emperoure sholde'. Now the symbols of sovereignty are conferred 'by the Poopys hondis, with all the royalté in the worlde to welde for ever'. It remains only to establish 'all the londys frome Rome unto Fraunce', for the ideal of sovereignty is expressed through a peaceful and orderly empire. Malory's idea of good government is implicit in Arthur's words to Lancelot and Bors:

> 'Loke that ye take seynge in all your brode londis, and cause youre lyege men to know you as for their kynde lorde, and suffir never your soveraynté to be alledged with your subjectes, nother the soveraynge of your persone and londys.
>
> (245; not in the source)

The quest for Rome, then, may be regarded as a symbolic action demonstrating the ideal of sovereignty. The good king is one who overcomes evil, establishes peace, and enjoys the allegiance of his subjects.

Arthur's early wars and his Roman campaign establish him at the pinnacle of a mythic society consisting of tributary kings such as Anguish of Ireland, Urience of Gore, Howell of Brittany and the King of North Galys (Wales) whose chief function seems to be participation in tournaments; of Round Table knights whose successful quests maintain order and justice within the empire; and of courtly ladies who inspire the knights' prowess. No account is taken of the lower classes[55] except when a knight requires transportation, food, arms or services related to the pursuit of a quest. (The exclusive and arbitrary ethic of romance is well illustrated by Lancelot's expeditious murder of the woodcutter whose cart the hero requisitions.) During the long *Book of Sir Tristram de Lyones*, the king's role is largely ceremonial as he presides over feasts, organises tournaments, welcomes visitors and commends deeds of worship. He refuses to participate in the Grail quest, foreseeing that it will deprive him of 'the fayryst and the trewyst of knyghthode that ever was sene togydir in ony realme of the worlde'.

When the linear biography is resumed, the integrity of the king's role as administrator of justice is tested three times by charges of treason levelled against his queen.[56] Having accused Guenevere of poisoning Sir Patryse, a charge of which she is completely innocent, Sir Mador appeals for justice to Arthur not as king but as fellow knight. This appeal, implying that chivalry takes precedence over sovereignty, does not occur in Malory's sources but it is consistent with his emphasis on the chivalric ideal of fellowship. The second charge, based on the queen's alleged adultery with one of the wounded knights, also revolves around the inter-relationships of sovereignty and chivalry as Meleagant 'ever cryed upon Sir Arthur to do hym justyse' (the appellation is significant). As it is impossible for the king to combine the regal role of judging with the chivalric role of defending a lady's honour, the wielding of the sword in the *duels judiciaires*[57] is left to Lancelot who turns up expediently. He easily defeats Mador, graciously spares his opponent's life and exonerates the Queen who has a right to his service because she had long ago saved his reputation. For, Lancelot recounts, on the same day that Arthur made him a knight

> thorow my hastynes I loste my swerde, and my lady, youre quene, founde hit, and lapped hit in her trayne, and gave me my swerde whan I had nede thereto; and ells had I bene shamed amonge all knyghtes. And therefore, my lorde Arthure, I promysed her at that day ever to be her knyght in ryght othir in wronge.

(1058)

The resolution of the second judicial duel is effected with less regard for chivalric decorum. Meleagant is undoubtedly a nefarious character and Lancelot gives him more than a fair chance, but in the end at the queen's command he is slain. Since Meleagant is a Round Table knight who has begged for mercy, the incident indicates the inability of even the best knight to keep to the code of the fellowship. This failure diminishes Arthur's power as the charges against his wife diminish his honour.

After the third charge, this time on the grounds of the queen's adultery with Lancelot, manifest guilt precludes a judicial duel and Arthur orders 'the quene to the fyre and there to be brente' for that, as Malory takes care to point out, was the law in those days. This significant change from the procedure in the *Mort Artu* and the stanzaic *Le Morte Arthur*, where Guenevere is sentenced to death by the barons, occurs not because Malory's Arthur is less humane but because 'Malory's conception of kingship tends to transform a feudal overlord into a fiftcenth-century monarch'.[58] The image of Arthur as an archetypal hero and *Christianissimus rex*, established in 'The Tale of King Arthur' and 'The Tale of the Noble King Arthur that was emperor himself through dignity of his hands' is now blurred by a fifteenth century frame of reference.

With Mordred's usurpation of the crown while Arthur is fighting in France, Malory returns to the matter and viewpoint of the chronicles[59] where the tragedy of an individual is subsumed by the *topos* of kingship. In Malory's poetic sources as well as in the *Mort Artu*, the iconography of Arthur's downfall includes the image of Fortune's Wheel. The polysemous Goddess Fortuna appealed equally to the medieval author, historian, philosopher, and artist.[60] Though she could affect the destiny of every man in matters relating to love, war, travel on land and sea, money, fame, and death, the motion of her wheel was most frequently associated with the fate of kings. For example, in the *Holkham Bible Picture Book* (London, British Library MS Add. 47682, fol. 4; ca. 1330), Fortune, a crowned and wimpled queen wearing a fashionably draped gown, is shown turning a four-spoked wheel. In the twelve o'clock position sits a king (identified as such by his crown and sceptre) beside whose image is written *regno*. On his right in the nine o'clock position, a figure with his feet twined about the wheel stretches out his left hand to take the crown (*regnabo*) while opposite him the *regnavi* figure, having already lost his sceptre and crown, hangs upside down as he clings for dear life to the wheel. Crushed by the wheel in the most abject position, a recumbent, barefooted, corpse-like figure bears the label, 'Sum sine regno'.[61]

Malory's English source, the alliterative *Morte Arthure*, provides the most extensive literary treatment of the motif, linking it with an equally popular subject, that of the Nine Worthies:

> The rowell whas rede golde with ryall stonys,
> Raylide with reches and rubyes inewe;
> The spekes was splentide all with speltis of silver,
> The space of a spere-lenghe springande full faire;
> Thereone was a chayere of chalke-whytte silver
> And chekyrde with charebocle, chawngynge of hewes;
> Appon the compas ther clewide kyngis one rawe
> With corowns of clere golde, that krakede in sondire.
>
> (11. 3262–3269)

In this poem, Arthur's fall is attributed specifically to his flawed character. The philosopher who interprets the dream points out to the king:

> Thow has schedde myche blode and schalkes distroyede,
> Sakeles in cirquytrie in sere kynges landis.
>
> (ll. 3398–9)

The *Mort Artu* also condemns the hero's pride. Having explained his situation, Fortune pushes the hapless monarch to the ground so roughly that all his bones are broken. The author of the stanzaic *Morte* and Malory omit the goddess, retaining only the wheel and its associated images.

Because Malory's attitude to Arthur is sympathetic, rather than condemnatory, and because his purpose in using the Wheel is prophetic, that is, historical, rather than tropological, he uses as his source the stanzaic poem which describes Arthur's dream vision quite simply:

> Him thought he sat in gold all cledde,
> As he was comely king with crown
> Upon a wheel that full wide spredde,
> And all his knightes to him boun.
>
> (ll. 3172–3175)

The black water beneath the wheel, the many 'serpentes and wormes and wylde bestis fowle and orryble,' and the sudden reversal of the wheel that plunges the king into the water where his limbs are attacked by the serpents are *Morte Arthur* images that create a powerful atmosphere of doom. Two original details in Malory suggest that he might have had a visual source as well – the king's garment, 'the rychest clothe of golde that myght be made', and the chair raised on a scaffold and attached to the wheel. The scaffold construction is very similar to one depicted in a fifteenth century translation of Boethius' *De Consolatio Philosophiae*, Paris, Bibliothèque Nationale MS Fr. 809, fol. 40, where the wheel is raised on a scaffold with a king's throne attached. In the miniature, too, the figure of Fortune is lacking. For Malory, the Wheel seems to represent the fact of Arthur's downfall rather than the cause. The Wheel's sudden reversal foretells the inevitable loss of the crown through usurpation and death.

The atmosphere of foreboding established by the prophetic dream is sustained by subsequent images; the adder emerging from the 'lytyll hethebuysshe' on Salisbury Plain, the drawn sword of the knight who has been stung, the marshalling clamour of trumpets and horns, the bodies of noble knights laid to the cold earth, Mordred leaning on his sword among a great heap of dead men, and the final exchange of deadly blows. Pierced by Arthur's spear, the usurper threste hymselff with the myght that he had upp to the burre of kyng Arthurs speare, and ryght so he smote hys fadir, Kynge Arthure, with hys swerde holdynge in both hys hondys, uppon the syde of the hede, that the swerde perced the helmet and the tay of the brayne'.

(1237; Malory's addition)

Then in the night robbers come onto the field to strip the fallen knights of their rings, broaches, and jewels . . . 'And who that were nat dede all oute, there they slew them for their harneys and their ryches'. It is a terrible exemplification of Fortune's power.

The impinging of supernatural compulsions on the Arthurian world is evidenced, not only by the operation of a fate which may be seen as providential, but also by the demands of the faerie Otherworld. The story of Arthur cannot be completed until Excalibur has been returned to its source. Malory seems to make a connection between the disposal of the sword and Arthur's survival. In an original speech, the king rebukes Bedevere for failing a second time to throw away the noble sword with its jewelled hilt and pommel:

'. . . thy longe taryynge puttith me in grete jouperté of my lyff, for I have takyn colde. And but if thou do now as I bydde the, if ever I may se the, I shall sle the myne owne hondis, for thou woldist for my rych swerde se me dede'.

(1239)

La Mort's Arthur wants the sword thrown away lest it fall into the hands of an inferior, while the stanzaic poem's king gives no reason for his command. Malory emphasises the cyclical pattern of Arthur's life, already suggested by the Wheel of Fortune, by repeating the earlier image of arm and hand emerging from the water of the lake and brandishing the sword. He also pairs the supernatural conception effected through the magic of Merlin and Merlin's reception of the newborn child with the supernatural departure for Avalon in the company of three fées and the Queen of the Waste Lands, a character from the Grail legend.

In the *Mort Artu* it is clear that Excalibur is thrown into a lake, while the ship carrying Morgan and the other ladies travels eastward across the sea. In the stanzaic *Morte*, Excalibur is thrown into 'the salte flood' from a place on the seashore where Arthur and Bedevere subsequently find the 'riche ship with mast and ore / Full of ladies'. Malory's presentation of geographic space is so vague that no distinction is made between the lake and the sea. However, he adds a number of visual details relating to objects in the foreground; for example, the black hoods of the ladies, the fact that one of the ladies was a queen (a status conventionally indicated by a crown in illustrations), the weeping and shrieking of the women, the vivid phrase 'in one of their lappis kyng Arthure layde hys hede', the 'lytyll barge' propelled by oars, and the weeping knight on the shore with the forest at his back.

The French authors, having little interest in the apotheosis of a British king, bury him at the Black Chapel in a splendid tomb. Selecting images from the stanzaic *Morte*, Malory sustains the elegiac mood by references to grey woods, a 'newe gravyn' tomb, a hermit grovelynge on all four', a midnight visit by several ladies who accompany a corpse, the burning of a hundred tapers and the offering of gold coins which Malory characteristically increases from a hundred pounds to a thousand bezants. The chapel tended by the former Archbishop of Canterbury is near Glastonbury, the place where Arthur's tomb was supposedly found in 1191.[62] At the same time, Malory evidently knows the venerable tradition of Arthur's survival in the Celtic Otherworld (Avalon).[63] His version of the passing of Arthur incorporates such Otherworld motifs as the beautiful supernatural women, the westward voyage, the 'locus amoenus', the idea of healing, and the possibility of the hero's return to this world. The puzzling phrase, 'here in thys worlde he chaunged hys lyff', may be explained by recalling that in the middle ages the Celtic Otherworld (fairyland) was considered part of this world, though protected by a perilous passage across water or through rock. A mortal who gained access with the assistance of an otherworld guide changed his life not only because he enjoyed paradisal entertainments free from trouble and pain but also because he lived according to a different time scheme.[64]

The equally puzzling report that 'he shall wynne the Holy Crosse' may have been suggested by the author's association of Arthur with his fellow Worthy, Godfrey of Bouillon, or with another romance hero, Ogier the Dane, who dwelt with Morgan le Fay in Avalon for two hundred years before returning to France so that he could save Christendom from the enemy. The story of Arthur concludes with a neat combination of the two endings:

And many men say that there ys wrytten uppon the tumbe thys: Hic iacet Arthurus, Rex Quondam Rexque Futurus.[65]

(1242)

2

Castles, Courts, and Courtesy

The castle, as Rose Macaulay remarks, has always been 'a formidable image, a powerful, intimidating fantasy of the human imagination'.[1] The supreme expression of *noblesse*, it denotes a privileged class separated from the rest of society by its occupation of a different kind of space. Its distinctive features have been described by Erich Auerbach in his essay on Chrétien de Troyes' *Yvain*:[2]

> The setting is fixed and isolating, as distinct from the mores of other strata of society, as is that of the *chanson de geste*, but it is much more refined and elegant. Women play an important part in it; the mannerly ease and comfort of the social life of a cultured class have been attained.

Within the castle walls is found a world regulated by the codes of chivalry and courtly love rather than by the political and economic requirements of real feudal life. The chief responsibility of the lord and lady is to provide the knight-errant with hospitality, entertainment, reward, and opportunities for chivalric adventure.

No doubt, the wish-fulfilling castles of Arthurian romance owe something to Celtic stories of fairy mistresses who entertained mortal lovers in Otherworld Castles.[3] In the *Serglige ConCulainn* ('Cuchulinn's Sickbed'), for example, are to be found such recurrent motifs as a castle of dazzling brightness, a hospitable host, a heroine of great beauty and power, a company of ladies, a feast copiously supplying food and drink, melodious music, an adversary to be defeated, and insanity resulting from the hero's eventual loss of his lady love. It is not difficult to see how the beautiful and terrible Celtic fées who enticed the Irish heroes Laeg, Cuchulinn, Conle, and Cael to a Castle of Maidens in Mag Mell became identified with the courtly ladies who controlled the destinies of Lancelot, Tristram, Gareth, and Lamerok. The otherworld castles where the mortal heroes are entertained are analogous to the hospitable castles which shelter Malory's knights after a day in the forest. In castles of delight they find warmth and security, feasting and love-making, 'all maner of gamys and

31

playes, of daunsyng and syngynge', and 'myry reste' at night. The very names evoke 'the mystery and spell of everything remote and unattainable', in W. P. Ker's phrase – the Castell Adventures, the Castell of Ladyes, the Joyous Gard, La Beale Regard, the Castle Blanke, the Castle of Maidens, Camelot. Although Malory describes no castle entertainments that can compare with those enjoyed by Gawain at the Green Knight's Castle or by Chrétien's Erec and Enid at their coronation, nevertheless Camelot, Kynge Kenadowne, Gryngamour's castle, and Ettarde's castle with its pavilions outside the gate evoke an aura of joy and glamour. Even the ascetic life of a hermitage can be ameliorated by the resources of a neighbouring castle, as the Lady Lyonesse makes clear when she sends her dwarf off to administer to Sir Gareth:

> 'Therefore go thou unto an hermytage of myne hereby and bere with the of my wyne in too flagons of sylver – they ar of two galons – and also two caste of brede, with the fatte venyson ibake and deynté foules; and a cuppe of golde here I delyver the that is ryche of precious stonys'.
>
> (318)

In addition to being a source of entertainment, the castle is a place of healing. A knight languishing because of madness, wounds, or love may be restored to health with 'good metys and good drynkys', as Lancelot is in the castle of Blyaunt. The healing powers of the Celtic fairy queen imbue with supernatural efficacy the salves which beautiful and powerful women apply to the wounds of Tristram, Gareth, and Alexander the Orphan. In such a way did the fées Fann and LíBan heal Cuchulinn so that he might fight for Labraid against his enemies. As A. C. L. Brown has pointed out in his analysis of the *Serglige sage*, a battle between the hero and a tyrant, either for the purpose of testing the former's valour or as a means of freeing the fée from an evil oppressor, is a common motif in Celtic stories of Otherworld journeys. Similarly, Malory's castles of delight retain an ambient bellicosity. Before Sir Gareth can participate in the 'good chere' of the 'whyght towre as ony snowe, well macchecolde all aboute and double-dyked', he must joust with and defeat the Red Knight of the Red Lands. In contrast, the doomed knight Balin first enjoys in a castle of ladies 'daunsynge and mynstralsye and alle maner of joye' and then is required to undertake a fatal combat with a red knight who turns out to be his brother.

The social setting of romance, centred in castle life, is not just a glamorised form of the real social scene with the draughts, dirt, darkness and dogs removed. Marvellous artefacts and excitements add dangers not found in real life. Mantles, drinking horns, and rich scabbards sent as gifts turn out to be magical tests or supernatural dangers. A ring increases a lady's beauty or ensures a knight's safety. A sumptuous banquet presages capture by a fée. A castle bed brings its occupant supernatural encounters. That several of the castles in *Le Morte Darthur* were originally Otherworld castles is suggested by

32

2. *The ladies of the castle watch knights jousting in the courtyard.* Meliadus
(*London, British Library, Add. MS.12228, f.213*)

such lingering traces of the supernatural as the giant knight and magical illumination that interrupt the 'clypping' and kissing of Gareth and Lady Lyoness in Sir Gryngamour's castle, significantly located at Avalon. The castles of Morgan le Fay must originally have been paradisal mansions to which the fairy mistress enticed her mortal lovers.

Marvels are not the most important aspect of Malory's settings. His practice is to rationalise some of the marvels, and to add realistic details in order to make them credible.[4] The four royal fées become medieval ladies who ride about protected from the sun by a green silk canopy and attended by a retinue of knights. Though Lancelot is brought to the Castle Chariot under a spell, he is imprisoned in a 'chamber colde' that is the antithesis of the Otherworld castles where the hero enjoyed warmth, light, and delightful entertainment, and he is given the unpalatable choice of taking a fairy mistress or dying in prison. Alexander the Orphan, another victim of the would-be fairy mistress, is carried to Morgan's castle, La Beale Regard, after she has given him a drink that keeps him insensible for three days. Morgan's cousin reveals that the fée's purpose in healing the knight and extracting his promise that he stay inside the castle for a year and a day is that he may 'do hir plesure whan hit lykyth hir', a suggestion to which Alexander vulgarly replies,

'A, Jesu defende me . . . frome suche pleasure! For I had levir kut away my hangers than I wolde do her ony suche pleasure!'

(643)

He is released from La Beale Regard by a realistic medieval siege which results in the castle's destruction through fire.

Like the Castle Chariot, La Beale Regard, and Gryngamour's castle, Corbenic must have developed from an Otherworld archetype.[5] When Lancelot rides out to seek adventure, he comes on 'the fayryste towre that ever he saw'; inside is 'a dolerous lady' who has been boiling in scalding water for five years because of Morgan le Fay's jealousy. The spell cannot be broken until the best knight in the world has taken her by the hand. The scene is evoked by means of specific images that set it apart from the usual generalisations. At Lancelot's approach, the iron doors unlock and unbolt, apparently without human agency; inside, the room is 'as hote as ony styew' and the lady Elaine is 'as naked as a nedyll'. When people have brought her clothes and arrayed her (the verb suggests splendid garments), she is the most beautiful lady that Lancelot has ever seen, except for Guenevere. The description of the feast proffered by the castle's hospitable host also has unusual features for it includes images associated with the Holy Grail. A dove that flies in through the window carries a little golden censer which fills the air with a spicey savour and produces on the table every imaginable kind of food and drink. A beautiful young girl bears a golden vessel, the Holy Grail, before which the king and all his guests kneel.

Since it would be inappropriate for the Grail Castle to serve as a castle of love, the supernatural woman Brusen, whom Malory describes as one of the greatest enchanters in the world,[6] lures Lancelot to the Castle of Case by means of a golden ring like one that Guenevere wears (Malory's addition). His belief that he is going to bed with Guenevere is also due to the effects of a cup of wine that Brusen gives him. It is only when he unshutters the windows next morning that the enchantment ends and he discovers the truth. While the French source comments didactically on the significance of Galahad's conception as a means of grace, Malory emphasises the treachery and the supernatural agency. Elaine is twice denounced as a traitoress and Brusen is threatened with losing her head for her witchcraft, 'for there was never knyght disceyved as I am this nyght' (796).

After being deceived a second time by Brusen's magic, a deception that leads to his madness and eventual restoration to sanity at Corbenic, Lancelot and Elaine with their child Galahad go to live at the Castle of Blyaunt, renamed the Joyous Isle. Elaine's father King Pelles has provided not only the castle itself but also twenty fair young ladies of impeccable lineage and twenty knights. When Perceval approaches, he sees on the other side of the water a lady with a sparrowhawk on her hand. The image suggests aristocratic pleasures in a setting isolated from trouble and strife. The ideality of the castle is increased by the lady's revelation that inside there live the fairest lady in the land and the mightiest man. But the castle of love image is undermined by the image on Lancelot's black shield of 'a quene crowned in the myddis of sylver, and a knyght clene armed knelynge afore her'. And every day, no matter how hard the ladies try to entertain him, Lancelot looks towards the kingdom of Logres and cries as if his heart would break. Ironically, his title, Le Shyvalere Mafete, 'the knyght that has trespassed', does not refer to his sin of adultery with Guenevere, but to his sin against the ideals of courtly love.

The only knight who is allowed to enjoy the company of his mistress in a castle of love is Tristram. Having come to England to escape King Mark's malice, Tristram and Isolde are installed in Lancelot's castle, the Joyous Garde:

> And wyte you well that castell was garnysshed and furnysshed for a kynge and a quene royall there to have suggeourned. And sir Launcelot charged all his people to honoure them and love them as they wolde do hymselff.
>
> (681)

But Malory is uneasy about allowing his heroes a leisurely pursuit of erotic pleasures at the expense of chivalric action. When Tristram goes hunting, he is armed and his men carry his shield and spear (Malory's addition) so that he will be prepared to joust with any knights-errant encountered in the forest. He regularly attends tournaments, urged to do so by Isolde who is careful of his 'worship':

> 'For what shall be sayde of you amonge all knyghtes? "A! se how sir Trystram huntyth and hawkyth, and cowryth wythin a castell wyth hys lady, and forsakyth us. Alas!" shall som sey, "hyt ys pyté that ever he was knyght, or ever he shulde have the love of a lady." Also, what shall quenys and ladyes say of me? "Hyt ys pyté that I have my lyff, that I wolde holde so noble a knyght as ye ar frome hys worshyp."'
>
> (839–840, Malory's addition)

Tristram evidently attends the Pentecostal Feast at which Galahad takes his place among the Round Table knights. 'And than sir Trystram returned unto Joyus Garde' and that is the last we hear of him until the report of how Mark murdered him with a 'trenchaunte glayve' as he sat harping before his lady, La Beall Isode.

In such fine French manuscripts as the Rylands Fr. 1 and 2, British Museum Add. Mss. 10292–10294 and Royal 14 E III, the artists delight in creating fairy tale castles with pink, orange, or indigo roofs, pale blue towers, orange battlements, and buff coloured gates, set on a green verge beside a stream filled with fish. They accurately reproduce such Gothic details as pointed arches, cusped and crocketted spires, chapel pinnacles surmounted by crosses, properly supported drawbridges, lancet windows in towers, and stone tracery on the windows of large buildings inside the curtain wall. Additional touches of realism include workmen with hammers and awls, carpenters building a boat, and a knight reaching out between the bars of his prison to pick a red rose.

Occasionally Malory composes his picture so that, as in a miniature, we view the whole scene. For example, as Gareth rides through the forest with Lynet,

> So within a whyle they saw a whyght towre as ony snowe, well macchecolde all aboute and double-dyked, and over the towre gate there hynge a fyffty shyldis of dyvers coloures. And undir that towre there was a fayre medow, and therein was many knyghtes and squyres to beholde, scaffoldis and pavylons . . .
>
> (308)

Malory's usual practice, however, is to refer only to those parts of the castle architecture that are relevant to the action. Ladies look out of tower windows so that they may view jousts and tournaments or give advice to young knights. Lancelot is put to sleep in a garret over a gate so that he will be able to slide down by a sheet and rescue Kay from three attackers. He rides into a castle courtyard, 'a fayre grene courte . . . a fayre place to feyght in' and ties his horse to a ring on the wall. Inside the hall, he finds sixty ladies who have been kept prisoner for seven years by giants and have been compelled to embroider silk to earn their keep. The castle turns out to be Tintagel, which, as Malory reminds the reader in an original identification, was once owned by the duke who married Igraine, '"and so after that she was wedded to Uther Pendragon, and he gate on hir Arthur"' (272). It is reintroduced here not for its historical significance but to demonstrate Lancelot's role as a righter of wrongs.

Certain parts of Meleagant's castle 'within seven myle of Westemynster'[7] are essential to the development of 'The Knight of the Cart' episode. It has a bay window from which Guenevere and her lady can see Lancelot approaching in the woodcutter's cart; Guenevere rebukes the lady for suggesting that '"we suppose he rydyth unto hangynge"' (1127). It has a gate which Lancelot forces open and an inner court where he angrily shouts out challenges. Guenevere's bedroom has an ante-chamber where her wounded knights lie on beds and pallets. There is also overlooking a garden a barred window that can be reached by a ladder. In order to gain admittance, Lancelot attacks these bars so fiercely that he bursts them 'clene oute of the stone wallys' and, at the same time, cuts his hand to the bone. Lancelot's blood which Meleagant subsequently sees on the sheets and pillows leads to the charge that Guenevere has slept with one of her wounded knights. Having accepted Meleagant's challenge to participate in a judicial duel on the Queen's behalf, the guileless Lancelot also accepts Meleagant's invitation 'to se esturys of thys castell'. But if the reader thinks that he is going to get a guide-book description, he is mistaken. As usual, Malory is interested only in a specific detail:

> And than they wente togydir frome chambir to chambir . . . And so hit befelle uppon sir Launcelot that no perell dred: as he wente with sir Mellyagaunce he trade on a trappe, and the burde rolled, and there sir Launcelot felle downe more than ten fadom into a cave full off strawe.
>
> (1134)

Particular architectural features of the castle, then, are used to effect the charge of treason against the queen and to ensure that Lancelot will be *hors de combat* when the time of the duel, eight days later, arrives.

Two more castle associations favoured by Malory because they lead to chivalric action are the 'custom of the castle' motif and the propensity of lords and ladies to hold tournaments. In 'Balyn le Sauvage or the Knight with the Two Swords' and in 'The Tale of the Sankgreal', the customs of castles are related to plot development. Riding through the forest, Balin and a damsel arrive at a castle where, as soon as they have entered the gate, the portcullis falls behind them and the damsel is attacked by many men. The castle has a custom that every passing damsel must be bled, for the lady of the castle can only be cured of her sickness by a silver dish full of blood from a virgin and king's daughter. As Malory foretells, the lady is eventually healed by Perceval's sister, who dies as a result. Three weeks later Balin and the damsel reach King Pellam's castle which contains the Grail relics. Because of a custom or *geasa*, no one may attend the king's feast unless he has with him his wife or his paramour. As a result, the knight who accompanies Balin is excluded and the hero is deprived of a companion who by lending him a weapon might have forestalled the Dolorous Blow. The final custom affecting Balin directly is the requirement that he must joust with a knight who guards an island. In complying, Balin kills his brother and is himself killed.

In 'The Book of Sir Tristram de Lyones', the motif is used to generate the kind of chivalric exploits that Malory enjoyed recounting but that the modern reader finds boringly repetitive. As an example, when Tristram is escorting Isolde to Tintagel where she will marry King Mark, they stop to rest at the Castell Plewre ('the weeping castle'). According to its custom,

> who that rode by that castell and brought ony lady wyth hym he muste nedys fyght with the lorde that hyght Brewnour. And yf hit so were that Brewnor wan the fylde, than sholde the knyght straunger and his lady be put to deth, what that ever they were. And yf hit were so that the straunge knyght wan the fylde of sir Brewnor, than sholde he dye and hys lady bothe.
>
> (412–413)

Tristram and Isolde discover that the custom has an additional requirement. If the strange knight's lady

> 'be fowler than is oure lordys wyff, she muste lose hir hede. And yf she be fayrer preved than is oure lady, than shall the lady of this castell lose her hede'.
>
> (413)

Tristram after making the conventional judgment, 'So God me helpe . . . this is a foule custom and a shamfull custom', challenges the lord of the castle, but Brewnor wants to hold the beauty contest first. In a vivid image Malory describes how Tristram 'shewed forth La Beale Isode and turned hir thryse aboute with his naked swerde in his honde'. Predictably, she is judged by the estates and commons to be the winner and Tristram loses no time in decapitating Brewnor's wife with a backhand stroke. The next stage in the adventure is the joust between Brewnor and Tristram for the possession of Isolde. Again, Tristram is successful; he thrusts Brewnor down into a grovelling position, unlaces his helmet, and smites off his head. At the request of the local population, Tristram lives in the castle for a while 'to fordo that foule custom'. And who should turn up but Sir Brewnor's son, Galahalt the High Prince, who has come to avenge the death of his parents. However, a reconciliation is effected, with Galahalt promising that the custom will never be used again. A similar proliferation of adventures results from the customs practised at the Castle Orgulus (463–466), a castle to which Tristram and Dinadan are directed by shepherds and herdsmen (506–508), and Morgan's castle where Arthur's knights, having been deprived of horses and harness, are imprisoned. The foulness of the latter custom is condemned by Palomides:

> '. . . this is a shamefull and a vylaunce usage for a quene to use, and namely to make suche warre uppon her owne lorde that is called the floure of chevalry that is Crystyn othir hethyn.
>
> (597)

In other words, the custom not only forms part of Morgan's ongoing opposition to her brother but also reveals that her character lacks courtesy and a sense of propriety.

An important adjunct to the hospitable castle is the tournament ground. Castle Perilous, the Castle of Maidens, Lonezep (a castle near the Joyous Gard), the Castle in the country of Surluse, and the Castle of the Harde Roche owe their significance to the fact that they are tournament sites. Occasionally, the tournament has a tenuous connection with the plot. Lancelot's release from Morgan's prison in the Castle Chariot is effected by one of those ubiquitous damsels who populate the landscape of romance. In return, the knight must fight in a tournament on the side of King Bagdemagus, the maiden's father. Lady Lyoness' tournament is devised, at Gareth's suggestion, to provide her with a husband and to reunite Gareth with Arthur and his court. At the Castle of the Harde Roche, Tristram appears bearing a shield that Morgan le Fay has given him:

> and the fylde was gouldes with a kynge and a quene therein paynted, and a knyght stondynge aboven them with hys one foote standynge uppon the kynges hede and the othir uppon the quenys hede.
>
> (554)

Morgan identifies the king and queen as Arthur and Guenevere; the reference to the central theme of adulterous love is obvious to the reader though the guileless Arthur fails to understand its significance, even when he is informed by a damsel of Queen Morgan that 'thys shylde was ordayned for you, to warn you of youre shame and dishonoure that longeth to you and youre quene'.

The tournament's chief purposes were the demonstration of prowess in a social setting and the assertion of chivalric virtues. According to Huizinga, the staging of the tournament in the late Middle Ages attempted to recreate 'the imaginary world of Arthur, where the fancy of a fairy-tale was enhanced by the sentimentality of courtly love'.[8] It is true that the events at the Castle Perilous have a fairy-tale quality, as Lady Lyoness' ring works marvels that she describes to Gareth:

> that rynge encresyth my beawté muche more than hit is of myself. And the vertu of my rynge is this: that that is grene woll turne to rede, and that that is rede woll turne in lyknesse to grene, and that that is blewe woll turne to whyghte, and that that is whyght woll turne in lyknesse to blew; and so hit woll do of all maner of coloures; also who that beryth this rynge shall lose no bloode. And fòr grete love I woll gyff you this rynge'.

> (345)

And so the hero is able to confuse his opponents because of his colour transformations. The glamorous aura of a fairy tale is also evoked by the articles that are offered as prizes. Marhault wins a circlet of gold, Uwayne a gerfalcon and a white steed trapped with cloth of gold, while the alternative to Lady Lyoness, should the victor be a married man, is a golden crown set with gems worth a thousand pounds and a white falcon. In spite of some pageantry, I believe that Robert Hellenga is right in concluding that 'the tournaments in Malory do not reflect the customs and practices of his own day but of the period in tournament history between the pitched battles of the twelfth century and the pageants of the fifteenth'.[9] Noel Denholm-Young's assertion that the thirteenth century encounters were intended as training for war[10] is borne out by the description of Lancelot's participation on the side of King Bagdemagus against the king of North Wales. First the hero smites down five knights with one spear, breaking the backs of four of them. Then he smites down the king of North Wales who breaks his thigh. His next opponent is unhorsed in such a way that his shoulder goes out of joint, and finally he gives Sir Mordred such a buffet

> that the arson of the sadill brake, and so he drove over the horse tayle, that his helme smote into the erthe a foote and more, that nyghe his nek was broke, and there he lay longe in a swowe.

> 263[11]

The extreme violence suggested by these images of dismemberment is ameliorated in the later chivalric contests drawn chiefly from the French Prose *Tristan* where the encounters have become more like games than battles. The catalogues of participants may produce an effect of chivalric plenitude but fail to engage the interest of the modern reader. The settings are sparsely created – a castle, a meadow ringed with pavilions, a forest, scaffolds to provide accommodation for the upper classes, and an elevated platform ('chafflet') where the judges sit. With monotonous regularity knights smite their opponents with spears that burst; shields are dressed, swords drawn, helms raced off. Similes from the rhetoric of battle or the hunt define the relationships of the combatants. Arthur likens Tristram to a mad lion, Palomides to a mad leopard and Gareth and Dinadan to eager wolves. Lancelot likens the unity of a company of good knights to the holding together of boars that are chased by dogs. Tristram fares among the knights as a greyhound among rabbits, while Lancelot becomes 'as wode as a lyon that faughted hys fylle' when he cannot find Tristram. Though the ladies are present supposedly to inspire prowess, little attention is paid to them.[12] Only Palomides, it seems, is so encouraged by the sight of Isolde in the window that his strength is doubled and no man can withstand him.

The most dramatic aspect of Malory's tournaments is not the jousting but the dialogue which includes discussions of strategy, speculations about identity, formulations of etiquette and comments on the relative merits of the top seeded knights. When Tristram, Palomides, Gareth and Dinadan attend the tournament at Lonezep all dressed alike in green, the similarity of their appearance creates confusion about their identity. However, they are distinguished from one another by the fact that they ride differently coloured horses. Lancelot and Arthur are thus able to devise a strategy of assault:

'Now chose,' seyde kynge Arthur unto sir Launcelot, 'whom that ye woll encountir wythall.'

'Sir,' seyde sir Launcelot, 'I woll counter wyth the grene knyght upon the blacke horse.' (That was sir Trystram.) 'And my cousyn sir Bleoberys shall macche the grene knyght upon the whyght horse.' (That was sir Palomydes.) 'And my brother sir Ector shall macche wyth the grene knyght upon the dunne horse.' (That was sir Gareth.)

'Than muste I', seyde kynge Arthur, 'have ado with the grene knyght upon the gresylde horse', and that was sir Dynadan.

(735)

The words in brackets exemplify one of Malory's most characteristic aims, the desire that what is mysterious to the participants should be clear to the reader.

The success of various knights in gaining 'worship' is more effectively conveyed by describing the reactions of the spectators than by describing the actions themselves. At the Castle of Maidens, for example, the lords and ladies cry 'The knyght with the Blacke Shylde hath won the fylde!' so loudly that, with the help of the wind, the noise can be heard two miles away. There are many exchanges about the impropriety of striking an opponent's horse and about the ethics of changing sides but the most important examination of proper conduct is Arthur's speech to Gareth after the Great Tournament:

'For ever hit ys,' seyde kynge Arthure, 'a worshypfull knyghtes dede to help and succoure another worshypfull knyght whan he seeth hym in

40

daungere. For ever a worshypfull man woll be lothe to se a worshypfull man shamed, and he that ys of no worshyp and medelyth with cowardise never shall he shew jantilnes nor no maner of goodnes where he seeth a man in daungere, for than woll a cowarde never shew mercy. And allwayes a good man woll do ever to another man as he wolde be done to hymselff.

(1114; original in Malory)

Though several castles in the *Morte Darthur* excite associations of prowess, worship, and reward, the most important ideal setting in the world of secular chivalry is Camelot. In his political and judicial role, Arthur holds court in London, Caerleon, or Carlisle. In his romantic role, he holds court at Camelot, the archetypal centre of the chivalric milieu. Despite Malory's identification of it with Winchester, it has no place in the historical tradition. English chroniclers do not mention it until 1580 when Stow cites Winchester and Camelot as two places where the Round Table was held. However, it was well established in French romance by the thirteenth century[13] and was referred to by a fourteenth-century Italian, Fazio degli Uberti, who claimed to have visited wasted, ruined Camelotto on an imaginary tour of Britain.[14]

In Arthurian romance it is a castle and a city, 'la plus aventureuse vile qu'il eust et une des plus delitables', according to the authors of the Vulgate cycle. Malory's Camelot is very different from the enervated court of the *Perlesvaus*.[15] Not only is it the scene of feasts and tournaments, and of the making of knights; it is also the source of Logres' power and the vital centre of the chivalric world. While the knight-errant's arrival at a hospitable castle or hermitage when day has ended provides an episodic conclusion to one stage of his progress, the final stage is not reached until the cycle of adventures has brought him back to Camelot, the beginning and end of his quest. Though every hospitable castle reached by the knight is an ideal setting, the hero's return to the 'ultimate' centre is an essential part of the secular myth. The annual reunion of the Round Table knights at the Pentecostal feast in Camelot is the single, unifying event of romantic time and place.

Unlike the way through the perilous forest, which is difficult to find without a guide, the 'brode way towards Camelot' is open to all. Tristram and Mark have no difficulty reaching the castle from regions of barbarism and treachery. Morgan, Morgause, Lyoness and Elaine are visitors to court. Knights and ladies seeking boons know where to make their requests. At court, Arthur distributes largesse and justice, drawing his sovereign power from the successes of his knights.

Violence is inimical to this setting. Early in the *Morte Darthur*, Balin is banished from court for killing the Lady of the Lake. Gawain is reprehended for his unchivalric conduct in slaying a lady and is enjoined to become the defender of the fair sex:

41

there by ordynaunce of the queene there was sette a queste of ladyes uppon sir Gawayne, and they juged hym for ever whyle he lyved to be with all ladyes and to fyght for hir quarels.

(108)

Carlisle, not Camelot, is the court associated with rebellion, war, and disintegration. Camelot is never mentioned during the Roman Wars nor during the final period of strife, both of which belong to the 'historical' rather than romantic milieu. The poisoning of Sir Patrise takes place in London. Morgause is lured away from Camelot before she is murdered. At Camelot even the treacherous Mark engages in a 'love day' with Arthur. Furthermore, Malory does not use the *Mort Artu* story that tells how King Mark destroyed Camelot and razed it to the ground after the death of King Arthur. The castle remains a symbol of wish fulfillment and timeless chivalric joys. In fact, joy is the emotion particularly associated with the symbolic centre. There is the 'mirth and joy' of the feast, the joy of weddings and love, the joy of joust and tourney held in the great meadow by the river of Camelot, the joy at Palomides' christening and at the coming of Galahad, and best of all, the joy at the return of the great knights:

And than there was made grete feystys, and grete joy was there amonge them. And all lordys and ladyes made grete joy whan they harde how sir Launcelot was com agayne unto the courte.

(833)

Camelot is the ceremonial centre of the Arthurian world. The harmony of the court epitomizes the harmony of the empire, a harmony reflected in ritual observances. Successful quests which begin with the asking and granting of boons at court protect Logres against external forces of evil and chaos, but the success must be publicly reported at court and the new-won knights ceremonially received before the ritual is complete.

The superiority of the Arthurian centre is stressed by comparing it with other courts. No knight of King Rions has virtue enough to break the spell of the damsel's sword but only a knight at Camelot. The mother of King Urry has searched for seven years through all Christendom 'and never coude fynde no knyght that myght ease her sunne' until she comes to Arthur's court. In particular, Tintagel with its giants, rocks, pounding seas and murderous king is the antithesis of Camelot. Unworthy boons are asked and granted there, faithful retainers are threatened, widows and their children hunted down. The horn of chastity is diverted from Camelot to Tintagel because, according to Lamerok, 'the honour of bothe courtes be nat lyke'. Cornish knights are consistently depicted as weak and cowardly, and defeat at their hands is regarded as shameful. Though Vinaver suggests that 'the references to the

42

weakness of Cornish knights are survivals of a remote past, and both Malory and the French prose-writer would probably have been at a loss to explain them', it is not unreasonable to suppose that a deliberate contrast is being made in order to increase the honour of Arthur's court.

The unity of Arthur's court is underlined by the unrealistic device of having the members of the court speak and react as one. Their joy at the return of the great knights has already been mentioned. Their mutal suspicion of Guenevere makes them stand mute when she is accused of poisoning Sir Patryse. They share the king's astonishment and shame when it seems that the queen will be burnt for lack of a champion to defend her against Meleagant's charge. The most moving example of their unified emotional state occurs when Sir Lancelot leaves the court forever:

> And there was nother kynge, duke, erle, barowne, nor knyght, lady nor jantyllwoman, but all they wepte as people oute of mynde, excepte sir Gawayne. And whan thys noble knyght sir Launcelot toke his horse to ryde oute of Carlehyll, there was sobbyng and wepyng for pure dole of hys departynge.

> (1202)

The image of Arthur's court defines the nature of courtesy which is a social grace, an expression of the good life in a material sense, and a virtue. It includes, according to Henri Dupin's study of Old French romances,[16] an antithesis between 'courtois' et 'vilain', that is, the idea of social exclusiveness; the performance of certain ritual gestures associated with hospitality; the moral qualities of loyalty, faith, generosity and compassion; an atmosphere of joy; an observance of 'mesure'; and the experience of that particular kind of love known as 'amour courtois'.[17]

Some aspects of the concept are particularly relevant to the roles of the king and queen. Guenevere is beautiful and gracious. She inspires the prowess of Arthur, Lancelot and many other knights. As a guardian of propriety, she imposes penances for discourteous behaviour on Gawain and Pedivere. She contributes to the splendour associated with courtly life by inviting twenty-four knights in whom she has great joy to attend 'a grete feste of all maner of deyntees' and she arranges that an elegant cavalcade of knights and ladies shall ride a-maying into the woods and fields near Westminster. The fact that both entertainments turn out badly does not detract from her *courtoisie*, the quality of which virtue Bors describes when he appeals to the lords:

> 'Fayre lordis . . . mesemyth ye sey nat as ye sholde sey, for never yet in my dayes knew I never ne harde sey that ever she was a destroyer of good knyghtes, but at all tymes, as far as ever I coude know, she was a maynteyner of good knyghtes; and ever she hath bene large and fre of hir

goodis to all good knyghtes, and the moste bownteuous lady of hir gyfftis
and her good grace that ever I saw other harde speke off.

(1054)

Malory does little to provide pictorial details relating to her physical appearance, her clothing, her jewellery, or her possession of such aristocratic signs as
a lapdog or a falcon. Yet the name 'Queen Guenevere' bears a weight of
imagery that operates on hierarchic, emotional, and moral levels, affecting
both the reader and the characters in the *Morte Darthur*, as Lancelot's lament
reveals:

'For whan I remembre of hir beaulté and of hir noblesse, that was bothe
wyth hyr kyng and wyth hyr, so whan I sawe his corps and hir corps so lye
togyders, truly myn herte wold not serve to susteyne my careful body'.

(1256; Malory's addition)

And Malory attributes her good end to the fact that she was a true lover in the
courtly way.

Like Guenevere, Arthur at court plays a ceremonial part, welcoming
visitors, presiding at feasts where his *geasa* at times prevents his participation
before he has seen some adventure. He grants boons 'well and graciously' not
only to importunate damsels and eager knights but even to Aries the cowherd.
His remarkable civility is displayed when he gives instructions that, despite
their insulting demands, the Roman senators should be

seteled and served with the beste, that there be no deyntés spared uppon
them, that nother chylde nor horse faught nothynge, 'for they ar full royall
peple . . . (and) we muste remembir on oure worshyp'.

(187)[18]

Arthur is much concerned with 'worship' (reputation) as an aspect of courtesy.
Such violent acts as Balin's decapitation of the Lady of the Lake and Gaheris'
slaying of his mother cause the knights' banishment from court because they
have detracted from its 'worship' by acting discourteously. But it is through
ceremonial gestures that are both simple and elegant that Malory best expresses the king's combination of *l'accueil*, *l'hospitalité*, *la bonté*, and *la douceur*.
Consider, for example, the depiction of Tristram's arrival at Camelot:

Than kynge Arthure toke sir Trystram by the honde and wente to the
Table Rounde. Than com quene Gwenyver and many ladyes with her,
and all tho ladyes seyde at one voyce,
    'Wellcom, sir Trystram!'
    'Wellcom!' seyde the damesels.

44

'Wellcom,' seyde kynge Arthur, 'for one of the beste knyghtes and the jentyllyst of the worlde and the man of moste worship . . .'

(571)

Arthur goes on to eulogise Tristram as a hunter, hawker, authority on etiquette, and a musician. He graciously asks the knight to grant him the boon of remaining at court, and he concludes by finding him a place at the Round Table in the seat formerly occupied by Marhalt whom Tristram had killed when he (Tristram) was Cornwall's champion. The entire scene is original in Malory.

While welcome, hospitality, generosity, and courtly love imply hierarchical relationships, another social condition frequently mentioned by Malory does not. 'Fellowship' refers to the organisation known as the Knights of the Round Table and to their shared ideals. Malory's first statement of the chivalric ideal is the oath which the knights swear at the institution of the Round Table, an oath renewed each year at the Pentecostal feast. They are charged by King Arthur

never to do outerage nothir morthir, and allwayes to fle treson, and to gyff mercy unto hym that askith mercy, uppon payne of forfiture of their worship and lordship of kynge Arthure for evirmore; and allwayes to do ladyes, damesels, and jantilwomen and wydowes socour: strengthe hem in hir ryghtes, and never to enforce them, uppon payne of dethe. Also, that no man take no batayles in a wrongefull quarell for no love ne for no worldis goodis.

(120; Malory's addition)

With its emphasis on loyalty, faith, generosity, compassion, and service to ladies the oath quite clearly can be subsumed within the definition of courtesy.

The term Round Table refers to a real piece of furniture, a social occasion, and a symbol. Belonging originally to Arthur's father, Uther, it is restored to the young king by his father-in-law, King Lodegraunce, as a wedding present. It holds one hundred and fifty knights who sit in chairs blessed by the Archbishop of Canterbury. The first Round Table in Arthur's court is attended by the hundred knights sent by Lodegraunce and twenty-eight found for Arthur by Merlin. When they have all gone to pay homage to Arthur

Merlion founde in every sege lettirs of golde that tolde the knyghtes namys that had sitten there but two segis were voyde.

(99)

One of these is the Sege Perelous. Destined for Galahad, it is the link between terrestrial and celestial chivalry. As new knights are created to fill empty places, their names magically appear. When Tristram comes to court, the seat of Marhalt, whom he has killed, is endited with letters that say, 'This is the syege of the noble knyght sir Trystramys'. The table accompanies Arthur from place to place, serving both as a roll call of the order – before the Tournament at Lonezep Kay discovers which knights are absent by looking at the names on the chairs – and as a symbol of the secular court. The social and moral significance is explained by Perceval's aunt during The Quest of the Holy Grail.

> 'Merlyon made the Rounde Table in tokenyng of rowndnes of the worlde, for men sholde by the Round Table undirstonde the rowndenes signyfyed by ryght. For all the worlde, crystenyd and hethyn, repayryth unto the Rounde Table, and whan they ar chosyn to be of the felyshyp of the Rounde Table they thynke hemselff more blessed and more in worship than they had gotyn halff the worlde'.
>
> (906)

The 'roundness signified by right' implies harmony, unified purpose, celebration, and peace. That the breaking of the circle will have disastrous consequences is well realised by Lancelot's supporters on the eve of his exile:

> 'For we all undirstonde, in thys realme woll be no quyett, but ever debate and stryff, now the felyshyp of the Rounde Table ys brokyn. For by the noble felyshyp of the Rounde Table was kynge Arthur upborne, and by their nobeles the kynge and all the realme was ever in quyet and reste'.
>
> (1203–4; Malory's addition)

As the fragmentation of the Round Table increases, the demonstration of courtesy diminishes.

The most detailed examination of the theme of courtesy is found in 'The Tale of Sir Gareth of Orkney', for which no immediate source is known.[19] The tale is set in the palmy days of chivalry, after Arthur has established his empire, but before adultery, jealousy and family feuds have corroded the fabric. The occasion is the high feast of Pentecost, the ceremonial climax of the year, when all the Knights of the Round Table (except those that are imprisoned or dead) meet together and renew their vows, and when Arthur will not begin the feast until he has heard or seen a great marvel. The *geasa* is a device that links Arthur's court to the world of knight-errantry, where worship may be achieved and the court's reputation enhanced.[20] The antithesis between *courtois* and *vilain*, words which have, says Dupin, both social and moral designations,[21] is illustrated by means of the hero-as-dümmlingkind motif. The marvel enabling the king to go to his meat is the appearance of a very tall, fair young man who is supported by two others. Arthur greets them hospitably by making 'peas and rome' and escorting them to the dais. In ceremonious language that is an indication of nobility, the young man asks that the king grant him one boon now and two more in a year's time. His immediate request is that he be given food and drink for the next twelve months. The courteous king, disappointed that he will have little opportunity for demonstrating his largesse, since he would never refuse food even to an enemy, urges the nameless youth to ask for something better, but when the latter declines to do so, Arthur turns him over to the steward, Kay, with instructions that he be given plenty of the best food and drink and treated as a lord's son. Gareth's motive, he later reveals, is to find out who his friends are. Certainly, he tests the courtesy of Arthur's knights. The discourteous Kay, on the grounds that if the youth had been of noble birth, he would have asked for a horse and armour, proposes to put him to work in the kitchen where he may eat enough broth to make him as fat as a pig by the end of the year. And in spite of Arthur's instructions, Gareth, ironically dubbed 'Fair Hands', finds himself seated at the far end of the table among the boys and lads 'and there he ete sadly'. Lancelot not only reproves Kay for his scornful treatment but, out of 'his grete jantylnesse and curtesy', offers to entertain Gareth in his room and later gives him gold to spend and clothes. Gawain also treats the kitchen boy graciously 'for he was nere kyn to hym than he wyste off'.

When Pentecost comes round again, the marvel initiating the feast is a damsel who seeks a champion among the noblest knights in the world. Inspired by the image of a lady in a castle besieged by a tyrant, Gareth petitions the king for his remaining gifts; namely, that he be granted the adventure and that he be made a knight by Sir Lancelot. The impropriety of a kitchen boy undertaking a quest is counterbalanced by the richness of his armour and the superiority of his horse that is trapped in cloth of gold as a sign of his noble lineage.

During the progress of his quest, his courtesy is tested in several ways. He must endure the taunts of the damsel Lynet who insists on defining him in earthy kitchen terms:

> 'Thou stynkyst all of the kychyn, thy clothis bene bawdy of the grece and talow . . . What art thou but a luske, and a turner of brochis, and a ladyll-waysher? . . . Thou shalt anone be mette withall, that thou woldyst nat for all the broth that ever thou souped onys to loke hym in the face'.
>
> (300)

She refuses to ride near him for he smells of the kitchen or to sit with him in the hall of a hospitable knight for 'hym semyth bettir to styke a swyne than to sytte afore a damesell of hyghe parage'. But his tolerance finally convinces her of his nobility 'for so fowle and so shamfully dud never woman revyle a knyght as I have done you, and ever curteysly ye have suffyrde me, and that com never but of jantyll bloode' (312).'

His courtesy is also tested when, after drinking wine and eating spices in Sir

Persaunt's pavilion, he finds the knight's naked daughter in bed beside him, an extreme example of the hospitable host's desire to provide entertainment. On determining that the girl is a virgin, Gareth refuses to dishonour her father by deflowering her. Persaunt concludes that the hero must be of noble blood. This incident may be contrasted with the later events in the Castle Perilous. A courtly ambience is created by references to games, plays, dancing, singing, feasting, and to a beautiful lady whom Gareth desires so passionately that he hardly knows where he is. This time the lady, who turns out to be Lyoness, is offered by her brother and this time Gareth is only too anxious to comply. The disapproving Lynet must use her supernatural powers to protect her sister's 'worship' until her marriage day.

In 'The Tale of Gareth' courtly love is included in the concept of courtesy and, to a greater extent than in any other part of the *Morte Darthur*, it is treated in a conventional way. Gareth's first quest is undertaken to rescue a lady who not only enjoys a noble reputation but also possesses 'grete londys'. Her persecutor, the Red Knight of the Red Lands (an unsuccessful courtly lover), is described by the damsel guide as one in whom there is not courtesy. The hero's prowess in the encounter with his opponent is increased by his joy at the sight of Lady Lyoness watching from the castle window. Both justice and mercy for defeated opponents depend on a lady's whim. It is the lady who defines chivalric virtues and rewards. Her decisions must never be questioned. When the lady decrees that her castle will remain inaccessible to her champion until he has laboured in worship for twelve months, Gareth must obey. The armed men guarding the gate, the raised drawbridge and lowered portcullis indicate that the lady is not yet satisfied of the hero's nobility. Instead of a hospitable castle, a poor man's house is his shelter in the dark night and there he has no rest but 'walowed and wrythed' with the pangs of love. After twelve months spent performing chivalric deeds of worship, during which time the lady discovers that he is a king's son, he wins her as a tournament prize and marries her at Arthur's court 'with grete solempnyte'.

The conclusion of 'Sir Gareth of Orkney' epitomises the concept of courtesy as aristocratic virtue and order. With the gracious king's enthusiastic approval, the betrothal of Gareth and Lyoness is arranged by mutual consent, rich rings are exchanged and the following Michaelmas is set for the wedding. The joy of the occasion is increased by the simultaneous marriages of Gareth's brothers Gaheris and Agravain to Lynet and Laurel, Lyoness' beautiful and wealthy niece. The symmetry of these pairings is aesthetically satisfying and, as neither of the ladies is ever mentioned again, we may conclude that they are here an expression of order. Hierarchical relationships are established by the arrival at court of the knights whom Gareth had defeated, each of them accompanied by a retinue to do 'omage and feaute' to their lord. The knights are given ceremonial importance by their appointment as officers of the feast – the Green Knight Sir Pertolope as chamberlain, the Red Knight Sir Perimones as chief butler, the Blue Knight Sir Persaunt as server, the Duke de la Rouse as wine steward, and the Red Knight of the Red Lands as carver. This is the only occasion when Malory distinguishes a feast by designating individually the honorary members of the king's household. As further witnesses to the hero's prowess and compassion, thirty ladies whom he had rescued from the Dolorous Tower turn up to do him homage. Hierarchy is again expressed as the wedding guests go in orderly array to enjoy the plentiful food, the revels and games and music – kings, queens, princes, earls, barons, and many bold knights, a completely aristocratic company.

The celebratory tournaments climactically reveal the greatest knights, all of them bachelors, for Lady Lyoness will not allow the married men to joust. Lamerok is the champion on the first day, Tristram on the second, and Lancelot on the third. On each day, too, the power of the Round Table is increased, as Arthur creates new knights and enriches them with lands. Thus through such ritualistic actions as marriages, feasts, tourneys, the expression of homage, the granting of lands, and the expansion of the Round Table, Arthurian *courtoisie* is made manifest.

The last great courtly occasion in the *Morte Darthur* is the healing of Sir Urry. Like 'The Great Tournament', this original episode was evidently devised so that Malory might maintain for as long as possible the ideal society described at the end of 'The Great Tournament':

> So than there were made grete festis unto kyngis and deukes, and revell, game, and play, and all maner of nobeles was used. And he that was curteyse, trew, and faythefull to hys frynde was that tyme cherysshed.
>
> (1114)

Sir Urry is a knight of Hungary who has been bespelled by a sorceress so that his seven great wounds will continue to fester and bleed until they have been 'searched' by the best knight in the world. Sir Urry's mother, who has been travelling for seven years throughout Christendom, has not succeeded in finding a knight to heal her son. Now she has arrived by chance at the ultimate court on the feast of Pentecost, the occasion when the Round Table knights have their annual reunion. There are one hundred and ten knights present and Malory names them all; the elegiac roll call summons up the memories of great deeds (and a few felonous treacheries) going back to the earliest days of Arthurian chivalry. The gracious king first attempts the healing, not out of pride but rather a desire to encourage the others, who follow him in turn. None is successful. Then as they all stand about trying to avoid embarrassment by speaking of 'many thyngis,' Lancelot arrives. Aware of his sinfulness, the knight is unwilling to attempt a test that the others have failed. But when Arthur urges him to do so, not from presumption nor in obedience to the king's command, but rather 'to beare us felyshyp, insomuche as ye be a felow of the

49

Rounde Table', Lancelot kneels down by Sir Urry, and facing eastward, prays that his 'symple worshyp and honesté be saved'. His prayer is granted and through God's grace he performs a miracle. After general rejoicing, the episode concludes in the traditional way with the welcoming of Sir Urry at court where he is richly clothed, with his success in a joust for a diamond, with the admission of Urry and Lavayne, Elaine's brother, into the fellowship of the Round Table, and with the joyful wedding of Lavayne and Urry's sister. But what makes the episode most memorable is the image of Sir Lancelot, weeping like a beaten child because the grace of God and His Blessed Mother still sustain him. From the reader's point of view, these tears foreshadow all the weeping that will accompany the destruction of the fellowship in the near future.

In this discussion of courtesy one should also consider the part played by the 'ceremoniousness'[22] of Malory's language. One need look no further than 'The Healing of Sir Urry' for examples of Malory's ability to create an elevated style that is appropriate to his noble characters. The words of address are ceremonious in their use of qualitative adjectives, often in the superlative form: 'My moste noble kynge', 'my good and gracious lorde', 'fayre knyght', 'my moste noble crystynd kynge', 'my moste renowned lorde', 'now, curteyse knyght', and 'A! my good and gracious lorde'. All these appellations have both hierarchic and moral significance. Then there is Malory's attention to gesture, a device used in the miniatures of Gothic manuscripts to convey the idea of courtliness. We are told that when Lancelot had dismounted and approached the king, he 'salewed hym and them all'. Lancelot's gestures of kneeling, raising his hands in prayer, and looking eastward are described, as is his handling of the wounds in ceremonial order; first, the three on the head, then those on the body, and finally on the hand. The use of repetition, with its delaying effect, enables the reader to share the feelings of suspense that must have possessed Arthur's court:

> And than sir Launcelot prayde sir Urré to lat hym se hys hede; and than, devoutly knelyng, he ransaked the three woundis, that they bled a lytyll; and forthwithall the woundis fayre heled and semed as they had bene hole a seven yere. And in lyke wyse he serched hys body of othir three woundis, and they healed in lyke wyse. And than the laste of all he serched hys honde, and anone hit fayre healed.
>
> (1152)

Sometimes, Malory's use of repetition seems unnecessarily complicated from the structural point of view but it does serve the purpose of emphasising Malorian values. A speech that in another context might have conveyed the impression that Arthur was a garrulous Polonius here suggests the weightiness of the occasion and the sincerity of the king:

And for to gyff all othir men off worshyp a currayge, I myselff woll asay to handyll your sonne, and so shall all the kynges, dukis and erlis that ben here presente at thys tyme, nat presumyng uppon me that I am so worthy to heale youre son be my dedis, but I woll corrayge othir men of worshyp to do as I woll do.

(1146)

D. S. Brewer has pointed out Malory's considered use of the second person pronoun to indicate various relationships.[23] 'Ye' is more distant and respectful, 'thou' intimate, contemptuous, or a sign of inferior rank. The king quite properly addresses Urry's mother as 'ye' and the formal pronoun is used in the exchanges between Arthur and Lancelot. But in speaking to the wounded Urry, Arthur refers to 'thy hurte' and 'thy woundis'. Field suggests that 'for the bereaved and the dying, emotion is too strong for etiquette, and the closeness of the pronoun is an attempt to deny the separation of death'.[24] When Arthur invites the healed Urry to take part in a joust, he uses the formal 'ye'.

Finally, something more should be said about the catalogue of knights that occupies a third of the text. It is an epic device which recalls heroic exploits, points out genealogical relationships, and evokes a mood of nostalgia for the good old days. Not only does it recognise the value of the individual (note the repetition of the words 'So ded') as part of a fellowship but it also substantiates the reputation of Arthur's court as the noblest in the world, in both senses of the word. Malory's digressions may seem a clumsy device yet they succeed in recreating a whole world of romance where good knights battle against evil knights and giants and wild beasts; where they are changed by evil women into werewolves or are rewarded by fair women; and some are lost in quest of the Holy Grail and some are betrayed. The catalogue allows Malory to make moral judgments which are, in effect, an assessment of courtesy. The severest condemnation is attached to the least courteous acts:

Also that traytoure kynge slew the noble knyght sir Trystram as he sate harpynge afore hys lady, La Beall Isode, with a trenchaunte glayve, for whose dethe was the most waylynge of ony knyght that ever was in kynge Arthurs dayes, for there was never none so bewayled as was sir Tristram and sir Lamerok, for they were with treson slayne: sir Trystram by kynge Marke, and sir Lamorake by sir Gawayne and hys brethirn.

(1149)

The catalogue evokes the glory of the courtly Arthurian world; at the same time it anticipates its destruction.

51

3

The Perilous Forest

The dominant image in the iconography of chivalric romance is the figure of an armed knight riding in a forest.[1] He may be accompanied by a few other knights or by such obvious guides as a damsel or dwarf but the most important relationship is the one between the wandering knight and the forest that exists to provide him with adventures. The hero carries into the forest such courtly virtues as loyalty, fellowship, and a desire 'allwayes to do ladyes, damesels, and jantilwomen and wydowes socour: strengthe hem in hir ryghtes', in accordance with the Round Table oath devised by Malory (120).[2] In addition, he needs courage and endurance if he is to accomplish the deeds of prowess that redound to the 'worship' of his lady, his order, his king, and, of course, himself. Gervase Mathew suggests that 'the perpetual sense of the forest, the absence of horizon' encourages the practise of 'a simple individualist code of ethics in which honour and dishonour had the sharp contrasts of heraldic colours'.[3] The forest renews the knight's vigour and fame by presenting him with challenges that mark the stages of a quest. Unlike the challenges of *la chevaleric celestienne*, these are external confrontations only. By overcoming evil knights, giants, and sorceresses, the self-confident hero exhibits chivalric virtues which he already knows that he possesses. The forest adventures reveal his strengths rather than his weaknesses; they enable him to progress socially but not spiritually. Furthermore, many of his opponents are fellow knights or knights who are Round Table 'material', as is illustrated at the end of 'The Noble Tale of Sir Launcelot du Lake' and 'The Tale of Sir Gareth of Orkney that was Called Bewmaynes'.

Like the castle setting, the forest of romance is an enclosed world, a 'Secondary World' of the imagination, in Tolkien's phrase, with its own kind of consistency and with 'a quality of strangeness and wonder in the Expression, derived from the Image'.[4] Malory's forest has little in common with the real forests of medieval England which, according to Oliver Rackham,[5] were chiefly of the pasture type, with a good deal of commercial activity going on in them. Even the sycamore, one of the few trees specifically mentioned by Malory, was apparently not introduced into England until the sixteenth

53

century.[6] The most important tree in the medieval forest, the oak, is mentioned as suitable for a chivalric rendezvous (277) and for tethering a horse (481). A high elm with its tangled falcon and rotten branch is an essential part of the scenery for it not only embroils Lancelot in the schemes of a treacherous lady but it also provides him with the weapon that he uses to knock out the lady's husband. The apple tree under which Lancelot is sleeping when he is discovered by the four fées belongs specifically to the landscape of romance for it provides a point of communication with the Otherworld, and, particularly, with Avalon, the Otherworld of Arthurian romance, which was called the Insula Pomarum.[7]

The force of the forest image is not derived from its botanical make-up but from its suggestion of limitless, uncultivated space, hidden menaces, and the kind of density that enables lead animals, damsels, giants, dwarfs, and knights to appear suddenly without warning. The density of the forest – or depth, to use Malory's concept – is appropriate to the Old French romance technique of *entrelacement*[8] since it allows several adventures to be carried on at the same time by one or more knights. While the pace of castle life seems leisurely, even static, the constantly shifting forest adventures produce a sense of rapid movement that is increased by Malory's insouciant method of expanding the topography. When Lancelot and Lionel leave court to seek adventures, 'they mounted on their horses, armed at all ryghtes, and rode into a depe foreste and so into a playne'. The weather is hot; the shade cast by an apple tree provides a good place for the knights and their horses to rest. So easily is the scene of an adventure set. When the damsel has released Lancelot from the Castle Chariot and brought him his armour and horse, he saddles up, takes his spear in his hand, and rides in a great forest all day without finding a highway but at nightfall he is suddenly aware of a red silk pavilion set in a glade. Later on, he happens to come into the same forest where he had fallen asleep under the apple-tree and meets in the middle of the highway a damsel riding on a white palfrey. Again, he rides in a deep forest for more than two days; on the third he rides onto a long bridge where he is suddenly attacked by 'a passyng foule carle'. Even when the hero has completed the climactic adventure at the Perilous Chapel and is about to return to Camelot for the Pentecostal feast, we are told that he 'rode many wylde wayes thorowoute morys and mares, and as he rode in a valay, he sey a knyght chasyng a lady with a naked swerde to have slayne hir'. Obviously, what interests Malory is the appearance of isolated adventure-producing images in the foreground. The reader is not expected to organise the moors and marshes, rivers, valleys, woods and plains into a complete landscape. In fact, as the following quotation indicates, the reader can only compose the foreground details into pictorial form:

Now turne we unto sir Launcelot that had ryddyn longe in a grete foreste. And at the laste he com unto a low countrey full of fayre ryvers and fayre meedys; and before hym he sawe a longe brydge, and three pavylyons stood thereon, of sylke and sendell of dyverse hew. And withoute the pavylyons hynge three whyght shyldys on trouncheouns of sperys, and grete longe sperys stood upryght by the pavylyons, and at every pavylyon dore stoode three freysh knyghtes.

(275)

The forest, low country, rivers and meadows are throwaway images. The bridge, however, demands attention as a conventional place of challenge. The three multicoloured pavilions made of silk and linen suggest courtly society and knight-errantry, associations confirmed by the mention of three white shields displayed on the shafts of spears, three enormously long spears set upright by the pavilions, and, finally, at each door three 'fresh' knights. The details are carefully arranged to provide progression and arouse anticipation. The forest exists for adventures and the adventures are signalled by specific images.

Tolkien's remark about the relationship between atmosphere and imagery can be illustrated by considering the 'contents' of the forest. What particularly differentiates this world from that of the castle (and from the world of our own experience) is not only the opportunity that it offers for questing and jousting but also its atmosphere of mystery and fear. Gareth's adventures with the 'colour' knights illustrate the use of figures in a landscape to present a challenge and to create a mood. On the second day after his departure from Camelot, the knight, accompanied by his contemptuous guide Lynet, rides through a forest until evensong when

they com to a blak launde, and there was a blak hauthorne, and thereon hynge a baner, and on the other syde there hynge a blak shylde, and by hit stoode a blak speare, grete and longe, and a grete blak horse covered wyth sylk, and a blak stone faste by. Also there sate a knyght all armed in blak harneyse, and his name was called the Knyght of the Blak Laundis.

(303)

Introduced in order of their importance, the images convey the idea of chivalric challenge while their colour evokes an ominous mood. Nothing is shown that is irrelevant to the action. The sense of objects isolated in space is emphasised by the paratactic structure which also lends itself to progressive description. Having defeated and killed his opponent, Gareth puts on the black armour and mounts the black horse, making himself an ominous challenger. In subsequent encounters the increased strength of the opposition is suggested by the proliferation of images, reaching a climax in the setting associated with the Red Knight of the Red Land – a huge sea-side castle 'double-dyked wyth full warly wallys', many pavilions and tents, 'muche smoke and grete noyse', large trees bearing the bodies of forty hanged knights with their shields and swords about their necks and gilt spurs on their heels, and on a sycamore tree, the greatest horn ever seen, made of an elephant's bone; the Red Knight of the Red Land has hung the horn there so that 'yf ther com ony arraunte Knyghte he must blowe that horne and than woll he make hym redy and com to hym to do batayle'. To the foreboding aroused by demonic images is added the wonder associated with fantastic colours. Though the Green Knight might plausibly blow three deadly notes on a green horn hanging from a thorn bush, and fight in green armour with a green shield and spear, his green horse has supernatural associations as do the Red Knight's red horse, the Blue Knight's blue horse, and Ironside's blood-red accountrements and steed.

The combination of fear and mystery is also evoked by Balin's forest world, a tragic and inexplicable setting where the ethic of the chivalric code is frustrated by the power of magic and fate. The hero's promises of protection are invalidated by the treacherous Garlon, who rides invisible through the forest, killing silently with a spear or inflicting wounds that can only be healed with his own blood. Balin's attempt to protect himself against Garlon's brother King Pellam leads to the creation of a Waste Land about the Grail Castle and a threat of vengeance. His offers of assistance to Garnish of the Mount, a doleful knight whom he meets in the forest, lead to more curses, a murder and a suicide. Yet Balin cannot be deterred from his journey through the forest by any number of unfortunate adventures or dire warnings. As he rides to his last rendezvous, the concatenation is overwhelming. First he comes to a cross on which is written in letters of gold (Malory's addition): '"it is not for no knyght alone to ryde toward this castel"'. Next there is the 'old hore gentylman'[9] who calls the knight by his personal name, Balyn le Savage,[10] admonishes him to turn back, then vanishes suddenly. The damsel, too, with her direct address and her warning about his shield, seems a messenger of fate. Perhaps the most chilling effect is the sound of the hunting horn

blowe as it had ben the dethe of a best. 'That blast,' said Balyn, 'is blowen for me, for I am the pryse, and yet am I not dede.'

(88, Malory's addition)

This metaphorical identification is a much more powerful image than the French association of the hunt with the pleasures of a hospitable castle. Aware that he is doomed, Balin persists in following the 'worshipful way' which has brought him little honour:

'Me repenteth . . . that ever I cam within this countrey; but I maye not torne now ageyne for shame, and what adventure shalle falle to me, be it lyf or dethe, I wille take the adventure that shalle come to me.'

(89; Malory's addition)

In fact, he actually longs for the inevitable end to his 'death ride': 'I wold be fayne ther my deth shold be.'[11] Alone of all Arthur's knights, Balin and Balan are swallowed by the forest from which they can never return.

Not the least important source of the forest's interest is its association with supernatural characters. Merlin and the fées are at home in this milieu, though they appear easily enough at court when an occasion arises. Originating as a 'wild man of the woods',[12] Merlin appears in the forest as a shape-shifter, a prophet, and an architectural engineer with the power of turning up unexpectedly, performing some task, and then disappearing as if by magic. The relation between creation and prophecy is particularly apparent at the end of 'The Knight with the Two Swords' where Merlin writes on the tomb with letters of gold, creates the Perilous Bed, makes a new pommel for Balin's sword, sets the sword in a marble stone standing upright in the river, builds a bridge 'but halff a foote brode' that can be crossed only by a virtuous man, and utters a number of prophecies that link this episode with the Grail Quest.

Merlin's sylvan origin is complemented by his end, 'putte in the earthe quycke' by the fée, Nyneve, to whom he has taught his magic. Nyneve excuses her imprisonment of the sage on the grounds that she fears him because he is a devil's son. Malory evidently finds the story of Merlin's infatuation distasteful for he greatly reduces and rationalises the account in the source.[13] For the magic tower of air under the flowering hawthorn bush and the lovely fée who holds his head in her lap and promises him her love Malory substitutes a stone-covered tomb from which the seer can never escape 'for all the craufte he coude do' but only by the art of her who put him there. All that remains of the magician is the voice that King Bagdemagus hears calling out and making sorrowful complaint. Malory's Merlin is a tragic figure whose great achievement in establishing Arthur's kingdom is undermined by a humiliating and destructive passion for a woman.

The fées are best regarded as descendants of the Irish gods, tall and fair, more beautiful and more powerful than ordinary mortals, and undisturbed by questions of guilt, punishment or judgment in an after life.[14] Like the Greek deities, they have no compunction about interfering in the affairs of mortals. In particular, the fées desire to possess a human lover and to indulge an emotion that may range from loving to mere lasciviousness. The intensity of desire is accompanied by an equally intense jealousy of human rivals. By means of a guide animal, a magic ship, or a fairy messenger, they may lure a hero into an Otherworld where happiness is imagined as feasting and love-making, though it also has elements of protecting and healing. Alternatively, they may themselves come into this world to entice, to rescue, or even to kidnap. As fountains (wells), lakes, and apple trees are points of contact between the two worlds, a knight-errant who stops at these places should not be surprised if he encounters the supernatural.

The Lady of the Lake is the first fée to play a role in the *Morte Darthur* where she is Arthur's benefactress rather than Lancelot's guardian. In the Vulgate *Lancelot*, she belongs to the forest, her lake being only enchantment intended to conceal her fair and noble dwellings. This concept is retained in the OF *Merlin* where we are also told that an underwater bridge allows the Lady to walk across the lake. Malory eliminates the enchantment and the bridge, telling us only, in Merlin's words,

'There ys a grete rocke, and therein ys as fayre a paleyce as ony on erthe, and rychely besayne'.

(52)

The simplification allows us to concentrate on the two spectacular marvels – the arm clothed in white samite holding a fair sword in its hand and the Lady walking on the lake, an image that creates a far greater sense of wonder than does the parallel passage in the French source. This is a good example of the English author's ability to improve on a scene by cutting away material that might distract from the central image. The fact that Merlin and Arthur must row out in a boat to take the sword further emphasises the difference between natural and supernatural while integrating the magic more plausibly into this world.

Morgan le Fay, Arthur's half-sister, is the chief source of baleful magic in the *Morte Darthur*. Unlike her analogue in the Prose *Lancelot*, she is here never successful in her designs. Although we are engagingly informed that she learned her necromancy in a nunnery, she is closer to pure myth than are any of the other characters. Hostile to Arthur throughout his life, she turns up at the end as an affectionate and beneficent healer; the paradox is explained by her possible derivation from two antithetical Celtic goddesses, the Morrigan, who was an Irish battle-goddess noted for her ability to incite destructive activities, to prophesy, to create effects of nature and to shape-shift; and the benign white goddess Matrona or, possibly, the water-born Morgen.[15] The wife of King Urien of Gorre and the mother of Yvain (Uwayne), she is also the lascivious fairy mistress of Accalon and Hemyson and the would-be mistress of Lancelot and Alexander. When she and her companion fées, the Queen of North Wales, the Queen of Eastland and the Queen of the Outer Isles, come upon Lancelot asleep under the apple tree, their splendour is not unlike that of other fairies in Middle English literature who come into this world to take human lovers. Thomas the Rhymer[16] sees a beautiful lady dressed in green silk and velvet set with jewels and riding a milk-white steed. Sir Launfal,[17] who like Lancelot sits under a tree 'for hete of the wedere', sees ladies wearing green velvet embroidered with gold and trimmed with fur; jewelled crowns are set on their heads. When Tryamour returns with her ladies to save Launfal from Guenevere's vengeance, the fées are riding Spanish mules.[18] Dame Herodis,[19] another mortal whose sleep under an apple tree brings her into contact with the supernatural, is later seen in the forest as part of a female fairy cavalcade – 'Nought o man amonges him ther nis.' Malory's description, therefore, utilises a common store of motifs associated with fairy mistresses but adds vivid original details. The four queens of great estate on their white mules are protected from the sun by a canopy of green silk fixed on four spears that are carried by four knights. Green has both generic and hierarchic significance; it is a fairy colour and a forest colour but, as well, it is the colour appropriate to queens and princesses.[20] By describing the fées as four queens rather than as the one queen and two enchantresses of the source,[21] and by including such specific details as the use of a horse-litter to carry the bespelled Lancelot to a cold castle dungeon, Malory produces effects of symmetry and pictorialism that make this scene more arresting than is the corresponding passage in his source.

While Morgan is the fairy mistress *par excellence*, associated with the Celtic Otherworld Avalon,[22] Nyneve,[23] also known as the Lady of the Lake or the Damsel of the Lake, was probably once a water fée but she has undergone greater rationalisation than Morgan or the Lady of the Lake. She has mortal relatives, for Meliot de Logres identifies her as his cousin. She is also a damsel in distress, whose kidnapping by Hontzlake of Wentland allows Pellinore to demonstrate his prowess. She evidently has no innate skill in magic, for she must inveigle from Merlin his knowledge which she then uses to incarcerate him forever. And far from adopting the free love practised by fées, she is, when Merlin courts her, a virgin, and later a faithful wife to Pelleas whom she first meets in the forest. She replaces Merlin as the chief guardian of the Arthurian court, saving Arthur from the fatal cloak, from death at the hands of Accolon, and capture by the enchantress Annowre, and exonerating Guenevere of the poisoning charge.[24] Her most vivid depiction occurs early, for she is the noisy huntress on the white palfrey who comes from the forest to interrupt Arthur's wedding feast as part of the adventure that Merlin devises to instruct and test the young court. In accord with fantasy's pattern of balancing good and evil forces, Nyneve is the necessary counterpart to Morgan. Her participation is less memorable, however, being confined to foresight and simple enchantments rather than to creating magical artefacts, shapeshifting, and devious plots.

Hallewes, the lady of the Castle Nygurmous (the name is derived by Malory from 'necromancy', black magic), is another formidable woman whose magic is introduced not as mere exhibitionism or mood making but as a means of providing a forest adventure that will test the knight-errant. The motifs of the fée's beauty, her desire for a mortal hero (Gawain or Lancelot), her hatred of a mortal rival (Guenevere), her contrivance of an adventure to attract the hero to the Perilous Chapel and the fatality of the fée's kiss or the fée's breath[25] are utilised here to produce a powerful effect of fear and mystery.

After riding for a long time in a deep forest, Lancelot comes upon a black hound behaving as if it were following the track of a wounded deer. The dog leads him along a bloody trail, through a marsh, and over a rickety bridge to a manor house. In the great hall he finds the corpse of a knight (Gilbert the Bastard) who has died of wounds, and his wailing widow. Setting out once more into the forest, Lancelot meets a damsel in distress, the sister of Melyot of Logres, who is identified as Gilbert's opponent. Melyot's wounds can only be healed by Gilbert's sword and a piece of the bloody cloth which is Gilbert's shroud. The Perilous Chapel containing these magical artefacts is protected by supernatural knights, nine feet tall, with black armour and drawn swords. Lancelot is warned first by the ghost knights and then by a fair damsel to leave the sword behind or he will die. Like Balin, he ignores the threats which in Lancelot's case prove to be the tricks of a sorceress rather than prophecies of doom. The sorceress Hallewes has contrived the whole setting so that she might satisfy her passion for Lancelot either by taking him alive or by killing him and embalming his body which she would embrace and kiss daily, in spite of Queen Guenevere. This forest adventure, which has no known direct source, enables Lancelot to demonstrate his courage, his service to ladies in distress, his fellowship, and his fidelity to Guenevere.

Dwarfs and damsels appear less as characters than as images facilitating the knight-errant's search for adventure. Though in Celtic mythology the dwarfs, often royal, were gifted with immortality, clairvoyance and the ability to disappear,[26] in romance they are generally ugly and malevolent, like the messenger 'with grete mouthe and a flatte nose' whom Morgan sends to Accalon or the servant of Phelot and Petipace who strikes Torre's horse. The damsel messengers are young, fair, and forgettable, except for the three whom Gawain, Ywain and Marhalt find sitting by a fountain in the forest of Arroy, a place noted, says Marhalt, for its strange adventures:

> And the eldyst had a garlonde of golde aboute her hede, and she was three score wyntir of age or more, and hir heyre was whyght undir the garlonde. The secunde damselle was of thirty wyntir of age, wyth a cerclet of golde about her hede. The thirde damesel was but fiftene yere of age, and a garlonde of floures aboute hir hede.
>
> (162)

The little scene has the elegance of a Gothic miniature or a fifteenth century tapestry.[27] Unlike the French source,[28] which makes the oldest lady the most important by virtue of alone possessing a golden circlet and a name, la Damoisele Chanue, Malory's description makes the ladies equal in importance and function but iconographically distinct. The old lady's garland of gold suggests honour and wealth, the second lady's circlet of gold suggests courtly sophistication, while the fifteen year old's garland of flowers signifies youth and beauty. The ladies are sitting by a fair fountain at the head of a stream, an appropriate place for an encounter between heroes and fées.[29] If the deep valley full of stones seems an incongruous image, one need only recall that a Perilous Passage, often a desert, conventionally surrounded the paradisal setting.[30]

When the knights ask why the ladies sit at the fountain, they are told it is to direct knights-errant to adventures. Each knight then chooses a lady who takes his horse by the bridle and leads it to the crossroads. After agreeing to meet at the same place in a year's time, the heroes set their ladies on horseback behind them and go their separate ways – Ywain west, Marhalt south, and Gawain north – through landscapes studded with such characteristically romantic images as a fair manor, a cross, a dwarf, pavilions, a giant sitting under a holly tree with many iron clubs and battle-axes around him, a castle filled with prisoners and treasure, and any number of bellicose knights and importunate ladies. Malory's story is more neatly patterned than that in his source since he allows the adventurers to meet again as promised at the crossroads and the fountain, even Gawain's lost damsel turning up, though she could 'sey but lytyll worshyp of hym'.

Time and again, a vivid image leaps out from the conventional descriptions of comings and goings. Pelleas gives instructions that his heart be taken out of his body and carried to Ettarde between two silver dishes. Bagdemagus, hearing Merlin making 'a grete dole' under the rock where Nyneve has imprisoned him, tries to lift the great stone but finds it is so heavy that a hundred men might not raise it. That strange, composite creature the questing beast with a serpent's head, a leopard's body, a lion's buttocks and the feet of a hart, and in his body the sound of twenty couples of hounds, pauses from time to time to drink at a well. Demonic images underline the perils of forest confrontations: prisoners beaten with thorns, knights bound with their own bridles and carried under their horses' bellies, severed heads dangling from saddle-bows, knights hanging head down from trees, with their gilt spurs shining in the sun. Mystery and terror are essential to the attraction and the challenge which are the forest's *raison d'être*.

The author of romance has several techniques for getting a knight-errant from the court to the forest, a journey that must be accomplished in such a way, says D. H. Green, that the audience's disbelief is willingly suspended.[31] Lancelot, tiring of 'play and game', simply makes up his mind to 'go seke adventures' and is off. An angry King Arthur dismisses Balin from court for his vengeful slaying of the Lady of the Lake. Morgan's son Ywain is banished because Arthur suspects him of complicity in the Accolon plot. His nose out of joint when Torre is made a knight of the Round Table before himself, King Bagdemagus departs from court vowing never to return until he has won enough worship to make him worthy of the fellowship. A fortuitous storm at sea on two occasions propels Tristram into the Perilous Forest. Intruders from the forest may break in on court celebrations, as happens on the occasion of

Arthur's wedding feast. In one of the liveliest court scenes in the book, a white hart runs into the hall, followed by a white brachet and thirty couple of black hounds in full cry. The hart circles the Round Table and when the brachet tears a piece of flesh from its buttock, it leaps over a sideboard, knocking a knight off his bench. The knight picks up the brachet, leaves the hall and rides away. At that moment a lady on a white palfrey arrives, demanding the return of her dog, but she is soon carried off by an armed knight. Relieved that the lady has gone 'for she made such a noyse' (Malory's addition), the king wants to get back to the feast. He is informed by Merlin (who has himself stage-managed the activity) that he cannot ignore these 'adventures' without bringing dishonour on himself and his celebration. Gawain must bring back the white hart, Torre the white brachet and the knight, and Pellinore the lady and the knight. Needless to say, they all ride away from court into a realm of adventure that contains not only the objects of their quests but strange belligerent knights, castles, dwarfs, pavilions, hermitages that provide little supper for the knights but grass, oats and bread for the horses, a lady who sits by a well with a wounded knight in her arms, and – an exotic feature – lions who devour the corpses of the slain.[32] The device of asking and being granted a boon, already discussed in Chapter 2, functions in much the same way. A character from the outside world enters the court for the purpose of leading one or more of the knights into the unknown.

Madness is the device that takes the two greatest knights, Lancelot and Tristram, into the forest for long periods of time. Victims of love, they become wild men of the woods.[33] As Penelope Doob describes him, the archetypal wild man is separated by physical features and particular habits from his civilized counterpart.[34] His skin is discoloured, his hair long, his dress made of foliage or skins. He is unable to speak or reason. His behaviour is rough or churlish, his food consists of roots, berries or raw flesh, and his lonely habitation is found in the desert or forest. Tristram's madness occurs after he has married Isolde of the White Hands and abandoned her so that he can return to La Beall Isode in Cornwall. Concluding from the queen's letter to Kehedin that she has been unfaithful – the double standard is neatly revealed in his accusation – the hero rides dolefully into the forest where

> uppon a nyght he put hys horse frome hym and unlaced hys armour, and so yeode unto the wyldirnes and braste downe the treys and bowis.
>
> (496)

By disposing of his chivalric attributes, his horse and armour, he is obviously rejecting both courtly society and adventure. He goes about naked, lean and poor in flesh, associating with herdsmen and shepherds who feed him, beat him with rods, and clip him with shears so that he looks like a fool. Nevertheless, his nobility is betrayed by his skill with the harp and the sword and he is finally restored to sanity, the courtly world, and La Beall Isode through the agency of King Mark, who rescues him from the forest, and the queen's little dog who, feeling a 'savoure of sir Trystram', leaps upon him, whining, yelping, and licking his ears, cheeks, hands, and feet until Brangwayn recognises him.

Lancelot's madness results from Guenevere's accusations after the enchantress, Dame Brusen, has tricked him a second time into sleeping with Elaine:

> . . . he lepte oute at a bay-wyndow into a gardyne, and there wyth thornys he was all to-cracched of his vysage and hys body, and so he ranne furth he knew not whothir, and was as wylde woode as ever was man. And so he ran two yere, and never man had grace to know hym.
>
> (806)

The thorns that disfigure his face and body signify his alienation from the court. Other details of the scene are supplied in Elaine's account to Bors:

> '. . . he toke hys swerd in hys honde, naked save hys shurte, and lepe oute at a wyndow wyth the greselyest grone that ever I harde man make'.
>
> (807)

The immensity of the wilderness into which Lancelot has disappeared is suggested by Malory's description of the quest which Bors, Ector, and Lionel undertake to look for their nearest relative:

> And than they rode frome contrey to contrey, in forestes and in wyldirnessys and in wastys, and ever they leyde waycche bothe at forestes and at all maner of men as they rode to harkyn and to spare afftir hym, as he that was a naked man in his shurte wyth a swerde in hys honde.
>
> (808)

When another twenty-three knights, including Gawain, Ywain, Sagramore, Agglovale, and Perceval, depart from court to search for Lancelot in England, Wales and Scotland, we see how the motif of madness can be used to proliferate adventures.

Lancelot's sufferings are also on a grand scale. He endures care and woe and pain, 'for colde, hungir and thyrste he hadde plenté'. He lives on fruit and water and whatever else he can get. Only his shirt and his breeks protect him from the sharp showers. After a demonstration of prowess with a borrowed sword, he is well cared for in the Castle Blank though the chains on his arms and legs wound him badly when he breaks out of them to help his lord. He is wounded again, this time in the thigh, when he takes part in a boar hunt. After being nursed by a hermit, he runs off into the forest again, coming by chance to the city of Corbyn where the boys beat him and throw lumps of dirt at him and where he lives under the castle gate on a bed of straw. It is King Pelles' courtly gesture of celebrating his nephew's knighting by giving even the fool a scarlet robe that leads to the recognition scene in the garden. Lancelot is restored to sanity by the Grail and to domestic life. Madness does not deprive these heroes of adventure, since they seem to acquire swords, spears, and horses quite readily, but it adds an element of pathos inappropriate to the knight-errant, though not to the courtly lover. Interestingly, the images producing the emotion of pathos are not dissimilar to those associated with the Crucified Christ in Gothic art – lacerations caused by thorns, an emaciated, almost naked body that has been beaten, wounded hands and a deep wound in the side. It may not be entirely fortuitous that Lancelot is healed by the Holy Grail.

Hunting, an aristocratic pastime, would seem to be a realistic method of providing transition from the court to the world of adventure but, in romance, it usually results in an encounter with the supernatural.[35] According to M. B. Ogle, the essential features of the stag-messenger episode are an apparently voluntary hunt of a stag that escapes unhurt, an encounter with a lady (a fée) at a fountain, and the union of the lady and the hunter.[36] When the castle image noted by Paton[37] is added, it is apparent that Malory's account of Tristram's father, King Meliodas, reflects a well-established romantic pattern:

> So there was a lady in that contrey that had loved kynge Melyodas longe, and by no meane she never coude gete his love. Therefore she let ordayne uppon a day as kynge Melyodas rode an-huntynge, for he was a grete chacer of dere, and there be enchauntemente she made hym chace an harte by hymself alone tyll that he com to an olde castell, and there anone he was takyn presoner by the lady that loved him.
>
> (371)[38]

When his wife Elizabeth runs into the forest to look for the king, she gives birth to Tristram (who is named thus 'to say as a sorowfull byrth') and dies. The unusual circumstances of Tristram's birth distinguish him from other Arthurian knights and perhaps account for his particular attribute of excellence in venery. This attribute Malory acknowledges when, in an original passage, he commends Tristram's skill in hunting and hawking, his knowledge of the terms and etiquette, and his setting of an example by which 'all men of worshyp may discever a jantylman frome a yoman and a yoman frome a vylayne' (375). It is not surprising that hunting is the device that on several occasions takes this hero away from Tintagel and the Joyous Gard.

The most significant hunts in relation to plot and characterisation are those in which Arthur engages. The first takes place early in his reign, soon after he has defeated the eleven kings at the battle of Bedigrayne. The kingdom is still in turmoil, with Saracens burning the countryside, slaying as they go,[39] and

3. Balin, the knight with Two Swords, meets a damsel in the forest. Huth Merlin
(London, British Library, Add. MS.38117, f.123v.)

the unrepentant rebels gathering their armies in the marches of Wales, Cornwall, and the North. Arthur has an ominous dream of griffins and serpents that wound him severely. To cheer himself up, he summons his knights and rides into the forest to hunt. Immediately, he sees a great hart which he pursues for such a distance that his horse drops dead. The hart escapes into the woods unharmed, as Otherworld messengers are wont to do, and the king sits down by a fountain (a motif linked with the supernatural in both classical and Celtic lore).[40] While drowsing in this faerie place, he sees the questing beast drinking at the well and then the knight (King Pellinore) to whom the quest of the beast belongs. In knight-errant fashion, Arthur proposes to take over Pellinore's quest and then to joust with him for possession of the horse that Arthur's yeoman has fetched. A horse, naturally, is essential to the pursuit of a quest. Finally, it is agreed that Pellinore may take the horse if he will meet Arthur in the same place at a future date. Arthur does return to the fountain in response to the news that a strange knight has set up a pavilion there and established a custom of challenging every comer. The fierce joust that ensues is depicted by means of such conventional images as splintered spears, spurred horses galloping full tilt, dressed shields, pieces of armour littering the fields, blood staining the earth, and the knights themselves, like two rams, hurling together so violently that they both fall to the ground. The pattern of quest and combat exemplified by Arthur's forest meetings with Pellinore provides the rhythm of knight-errantry.

The pursuit of the hart to the fountain and the joust with Pellinore have profounder significances, however, than those associated with demonstrations of prowess and discussions of quests. As Arthur sits in a reverie, waiting for another horse to be brought, he is approached by Merlin disguised as a fourteen year old child[41] who tells him that his parents were Uther and Igraine. The truth of the child's declaration is reaffirmed by Merlin, now disguised as an eighty-year-old man. In addition, the king learns that he has incestuously fathered a child that will destroy him and his knights, that he will die in battle, and that Merlin will have a shameful death, 'putte in the erthe quycke' but the king will die 'a worshipfull dethe'. Thus Arthur's whole life is comprehended within the bounds of revelation and prophecy at the fountain in the forest. The joust with Pellinore also has extraordinary results. Arthur's sword, presumably Excalibur, is broken in the fight and without Merlin's intervention he would have been killed. The final stage of the stag-messenger pattern, though delayed by these other adventures, is achieved when Arthur meets the Lady of the Lake, a fée who gives him the Otherworld gift of a new sword to replace the one that has broken and a magical scabbard of great beauty.

On the second occasion when Arthur's hunting brings him into contact with the supernatural, the stag motif is combined with the magic ship, another device for bringing a hero to a fée.[42] The original motivation, the desire for a mortal lover, has been distorted and expanded into a three-branched adventure illustrating three kinds of relationships that a mortal might have with Morgan le Fay. Of the three hunters who follow the hart so quickly that they are soon ten miles ahead of their companions, one is King Urien, Morgan's husband, another is Accolon, her lover, and the third is Arthur, her brother and the chief object of her hatred. Near the bank where the deer has been run to earth, they find a little ship with silken sails that has a number of paradisal features – silken hangings, light of supernatural brilliance, twelve beautiful damsels who call the king by name, a richly arrayed banquet table where they are served all the wines and meats they can think of, and the richest bedrooms with the most comfortable beds imaginable. It is a nautical equivalent of the Otherworld castle. But when they waken they find that it has all been a trick, for King Urien is back in Camelot in the arms of his wife, King Arthur is in a dark prison, 'heryng aboute hym many complayntes of wofull knyghtes', and Accolon is on the edge of a deep well, in great peril. The subsequent battle between Arthur and Accolon, devised by Morgan to bring about her brother's death, and the resolution with Nyneve's help, establish Arthur's chivalric quality by allowing him to demonstrate prowess, nobility, courage, endurance, mercy, justice, and generosity. Even his opponent ends by describing him as the greatest man of prowess and worship in the world. The two deer hunts reveal that Arthur is a paramount figure in the world of knight-errantry, though he still needs his supernatural helpers.

In the forest, knights are guided by 'aventure' or grace or fortune to take the 'right way'. They unquestioningly accept directions offered by damsels, dwarfs, and signposted crosses. It is taken for granted that following the adventurous way will increase one's worship. Sir Tristram trustingly allows a damsel of Morgan le Fay to lead him towards a trap because she promises him

> that he sholde wynne grete worshyp of a knyght aventures that ded much harme in all that contrey.
>
> (510)

So governed by destiny is a knight that his intentions cannot subvert his fate. Take the case of Alexander the Orphan:

> So was Alysaundir purposed to ryde to London, by the counceyle of sir Trystram, to sir Launcelot. And by fortune he wente aftir the seesyde, and rode wronge.
>
> (639)

The change of direction brings him to Morgan le Fay. By encountering and overcoming her evil designs, Alexander is initiated into a daemonic world that proves his powers and enables him to restore moral order. Palomides rides 'as adventures wolde gyde him' or 'whereas fortune lad hym', seeking Tristram or following the mysterious beast. Tristram more than once is buffeted by a fortuitous storm which blows his ship to a propitious place. An obsessive reluctance to be diverted from the right way is exhibited by Lancelot when he refuses to accompany Tristram to his castle:

> 'Wyte you well,' seyde sir Launcelot, 'I may nat ryde wyth you, for I have many dedis to do in other placys, that at this tyme I may nat abyde wyth you'.
>
> (778)

The vagueness of Lancelot's excuse is explained by the fact that a knight-errant need not know in advance the object of his quest.

Movement in the forest produces a cyclical rather than a linear effect. Knights customarily set out from a particular place on the perimeter of a large circle – for example, Camelot, London, Tintagel, Joyous Gard, – where kings hold court and ladies wait for the knights' return. Within the large circle are smaller ones, centred on a well, a castle, a hermitage. Since some knights move clockwise and others counter-clockwise, the meetings resemble those in the 'allemande left' of a square dance, with one joust succeeding another until the hero is reunited with his original companion. A series of incidents in *The Book of Sir Tristram* illustrates this movement. Tristram is travelling from Brittany to Tintagel on the outer circle (the sea) when he is projected by a storm into the Foreyste Perelus. Telling Brangwan and Governail to wait ten days, he rides off with Kehedin. They have gone only a mile within the forest when they see 'a lykely knyght syttyng armed by a well'. He wounds Kehedin and fights Tristram to a draw before revealing that he is Sir Lamerok. Their chivalric interchange is interrupted by another pair of travellers on the circuit, the questing beast and Palomides:

> And to breff thys mater, he smote downe sir Trystramys and sir Lamorak bothe with one speare, and so he departed aftir the Beste Glatyssaunte . . .
>
> (484)

Tristram and Lamerok take Kehedin to a foresters' lodge, then ride off in opposite directions to look for Palomides. Lamerok meets in succession, Meleagant making 'wofull complaynte' over Guenevere, two knights 'hovyng undir the woodshaw' to ambush Lancelot, and Lancelot himself. Moving on, he meets Meleagant for the second time and then Lancelot (there is a pause while they all fight to prove the superiority of their respective ladies) and finally Arthur who has been enticed into the forest by the enchantress Annoure. Meanwhile, in another part of the forest Sir Tristram encounters successively Kay, Brandelis, Tor, the Lady of the Lake, Arthur whom he rescues from Annoure and her knights, and finally Ector.

And than at a day sette sir Trystramys and sir Lamerok mette at a welle, and than they toke sir Keyhydyns at the fosters house, and so they rode with hym to the ship where they leffte dame Brangwayne and Governayle. And so they sayled into Cornuayle all hole togydirs.

(492)

Although all may seem chance and confusion, some sort of order is generally maintained. The dominant organising principle, of course, is the quest. It combines the progress of a journey – which may take on the nature of a procession as damsels, dwarfs, squires, rescued ladies or fellow knights are brought in to accompany the hero – with the *en place* rituals of a combat, an action which enables the hero to establish or maintain order. While travelling in the forest, 'a fertile world of ritual',[43] the knight encounters a number of similar obstacles. He overcomes each in the same way, by feats of arms, until a climactic victory enables him to return home. The 'custom' of a castle, the refusal to reveal one's name, the hurling of insults, the blowing of a horn, or the striking of a basin are stock motifs for initiating combat. The revelation of identity, the opening of prisons, the abrogation of evil customs, and the acceptance of Arthur's authority ritually conclude the combat just as the recognition at Arthur's court ritually concludes the quest.

Each day's stage in the progress of the questing knight ends, if possible, with his arrival at a hospitable castle. The frequency with which forest and castle are combined suggests that these images represent the antitheses between action and rest, danger and security, combat and concord, pursuit and achievement, primitivism and civilization, nature and society. No matter how long the knight tarries in the forest or how often he accepts hospitality in temporary shelters, he must eventually return to the court. The conclusion of *The Noble Tale of Sir Launcelot du Lake* illustrates the reasons for this desirable event which usually occurs at Pentecost. Since Lancelot appears wearing Kay's armour, Gawain, Ywain, Sagramore and Ector realise that it was he and not the inferior knight who had knocked them all down with one spear. This outcome is so gratifying that they laugh and smile. Then the knights whom Lancelot had freed from Tarquin turn up to honour the hero, with Gaheris providing a blow by blow description of Lancelot's prowess. One by one all the adventures are described by those who have benefited from the knight-errant's prowess, courtesy, courage, and mercy. Some of the defeated, at the request of Sir Lancelot, are made knights of the Round Table. 'And so at that tyme sir Launcelot had the grettyste name of ony knyght of the worlde, and moste he was honoured of hyghe and lowe'.

4

The way to Corbenic

No matter what theory one holds about the origin of the Grail legends, the version found in Malory's source, *La Queste del Saint Graal*,[1] is designed to express Catholic ideas of grace and sacramental ritual, virtue and vice, fellowship and solitude, human and divine love. The author brilliantly combines images of chivalric romance with the iconography of Christian art.[2] The result is a transformed view of the good life, as knights-errant, importunate ladies, castles, perilous forests, supernatural ships, enticing pavilions, marvelous swords and emblazoned shields take on a new sense. While the adventures of *la chevalerie terriene* are, to a considerable degree, wish-fulfilling fantasies, the adventures of *la chevalerie celestienne* provide exemplary models for daily life.

From the beginning, King Arthur realises that the Quest of the Holy Grail differs from the previous knightly adventures in which he has rejoiced. He sorrowfully denounces Gawain's initiation of this quest:

> Ye have berauffte me the fayryst and the trewyst of knyghthode that ever was sene togydir in ony realme of the worlde. For whan they departe frome hense I am sure they all shall never mete more togydir in thys worlde, for they shall dye many in the queste.
>
> (866)

The forest into which the knights ride – each choosing his own way as free will permits – resembles the *silva oscura* in which Dante finds himself at the beginning of the *Divine Comedy*. Both signify the sinful and precarious world of man. Angels and devils, God and the devil enter it to guide the Christian along the right path or to entice him into the byways of sin. Imagery is developed according to aesthetic patterns based on Biblical exegesis with the result that the view of reality is essentially symbolic. As Emile Mâle puts it:

> All being holds in its depths the reflection of the sacrifice of Christ, the image of the Church and of the virtues and vices. The material and the spiritual world are one.[3]

69

The effort of medieval man to apprehend divinity was complicated by two conflicting views of God:

> The one God was the goal of the 'way up,' of that ascending process by which the finite soul, turning from all created things, took its way back to the immutable Perfection, in which alone it could find rest. The other God was the source and the informing energy of that descending process by which being flows through all the levels of possibility down to the very lowest.[4]

Both aspects are exemplified in Malory's romance and in his source. The contemplative and contemplated God, 'an apotheosis of unity, self-sufficiency, and quietude',[5] is the object of the Grail quest, apprehended in part at Corbenic, achieved fully by Galahad in the spiritual palace of Sarras, a *figura* of Heaven. The energetic God through the agency of angels, hermits, virgins and disembodied voices intervenes in human life and creates the marvelous artifacts which arouse the sense of wonder.

At the summit of the celestial hierarchy is the Trinity. The iconography of medieval art has greatly influenced the depiction of Deity in romance. Until the twelfth century, the person of God was indicated by means of a hand or arm, a bright light, a fire or a sword. In oral and written tradition a disembodied voice also represented His presence. Several of these images are combined in the adventure of Ector and Gawain at the ruined chapel. As they sit talking, they see a hand and arm clothed to the elbow in red samite (the colour of fire). Within the bridled fist a great candle burns brightly. As the apparition vanishes into the chapel, a voice warns them that they can never achieve the Grail quest, for the bridle (abstinence) and the candle (right living) have failed them. The sword symbol is used to indicate the presence of God at Corbenic where Bors sees

> a swerde lyke sylver, naked, hovynge over hys hede, and the clyernes thereof smote in hys yghen, that as at that tyme sir Bors was blynde.
>
> (802)

At the same time, a disembodied voice orders him to leave the Grail chamber since he is not yet worthy. The sword image is powerfully used again when the weapon mended by Galahad rises up, great and marvellous and full of heat so that many men fall for dread. A voice then dismisses from the Grail feast all but the chosen knights.[6] A later aesthetic tradition is represented in Lancelot's vision of the old man with the company of angels who descends through an opening in the clouds to bless Lancelot's ancestors. This conception of God is derived from the Biblical image of 'the Ancient of days'. Finally, it may be the hand of God that appears at Sarras to take up the Grail and lance and carry them to heaven.

70

The iconography of Christ comprises a large number of symbols as well as representations in human form. The lamb, the lion, the pelican, the fish, the lily, the hart, the vine and the candle are familiar motifs and most of them are utilized by the authors of *La Queste del Saint Graal*. For example, Bors sees on a dead tree a pelican surrounded by young birds that had died of hunger. With the blood from its pierced breast the bird restores its young to life, dying in their place. The image symbolizes Christ, the Redeemer.[7] Christ with the four Evangelists appears to the Grail knights and Perceval's sister who in a waste forest encounter 'a whyght herte which four lyons lad'. During the celebration of mass which follows, the hart becomes a man while the four lions appear as a man, a lion, an eagle and an ox.[8] After the consecration Christ reassumes the white skin of the hart (representing the Resurrection) and escapes through a glass window without breaking it (the paradox of the Incarnation).

Of great interest to the thirteenth century was the doctrine of transubstantiation which had been promulgated as official dogma by the Lateran Council in 1215. The iconographic representation of the dogma is an original feature of *La Queste*, which was probably written by Cistercian monks[9] between 1215 and 1230. In the Roman mass

> the uttering of the words of the consecration signifies Christ himself speaking in the first person, his living presence in the *corpus mysticum* of priest, congregation, bread, wine, and incense which together form the mystical unity offered for sacrifice.[10]

The embodiment of this idea in image occurs several times in Malory and his source. From the doorway of the Grail Chapel at Corbenic, Lancelot sees the Holy Vessel standing under a canopy of scarlet samite on a silver table surrounded by ministering angels. At the elevation of the Host

> hit semed to sir Launcelot that above the prystis hondys were three men, whereof the two put the yongyste by lyknes betwene the prystes hondis.
>
> (1015)

When the successful Grail knights assemble in the hall at Corbenic, they are served mass by Joseph, the first bishop of Christendom who had been dead for more than three hundred years:

> and than he toke an obley which was made in lyknesse of brede. And at the lyftyng up there cam a vigoure in lyknesse of a chylde, and the vysayge was as rede and as bryght os ony fyre, and smote hymselff into the brede, that all they saw hit that the brede was fourmed of a fleyshely man.
>
> (1029)

71

At Sarras, Galahad who has been crowned king and is soon to die, sees a man like a bishop, surrounded by angels 'as hit had bene Jesu Cryste hymselff'; the man (Joseph) takes 'oure Lordes Body' between his hands and offers it to Galahad.

The most important image of Christ, however, is Galahad who is not a realistic character so much as a type of perfection. He is not a personification of Christ but a *figura*, one who shows in retrospect what Christ's life on earth was like.[11] Like Christ he is descended from David. He possesses a physical and moral purity that has never been tempted and cannot be defeated. He is protected by angels so that the devil is powerless against him. His coming has been prophesied far in advance by Merlin (as the Old Testament prophets foretold the Messiah) and a place at the Round Table has been prepared for him – the Sege Perilous which only he can occupy. That the events of his quest deliberately parallel the life of Christ is made clear by the author of *La Queste*.[12] By reducing the exegetical commentary, Malory suppresses and obscures some of the correspondences, retaining, nevertheless, the Messianic concept and the miracles as well as some parallels to Biblical history. The view of Galahad as a long-waited liberator is apparent in the Castle of Maidens adventure, the healing of the blind King Mordrain (a Simeon type) and of the Maimed King, and in the restoration of the Waste Land – events which combine Christian allegory with Celtic myth.[13] The miracles which prove his supernatural powers include the healing of the cripple at Sarras, the driving out of a devil, and the release of souls from the burning tomb (a Harrowing of Hell analogue).[14] The crowning of Galahad in Sarras recalls Christ's triumphant entry on Palm Sunday as well as the historical fact of the Crusader Kings. Finally, the elevation of Galahad's soul to heaven 'in the syght of hys two felowis' suggests the ascension of Christ as the apostles watched. The analogy of Galahad as a type of Christ is evident not only in character and event but also in imagery. The crown of gold rather than the crown of thorns often appeared in early medieval depictions of the Crucifixion;[15] a crown of gold rests on the bed on the Ship of Solomon where Galahad will lie to figure the sacrifice on the *lectulus* of the cross.[16] The lion image which represented the risen Christ[17] is applied to Galahad when his father reads a prophecy on the tomb at Corbenic:

'Here shall com a lybarde of kynges blood and he shall sle this serpente. And this lybarde shall engendir a lyon in this forayne contrey whyche lyon shall passe all other knyghtes'.

(793)

Later the lion in Lancelot's genealogical vision is identified as Galahad.

Since the third aspect of the Trinity, the Holy Ghost, is like the Grail in being an instrument of grace, it is of particular importance to the Grail knights. When Perceval's sister recounts the history of Solomon's Ship, she reveals that the Holy Ghost had prophesied to Solomon the coming of the Virgin Mary and Christ, 'laste of youre bloode, and He shall be as good a knyght as deuke Josue'. This prophecy corresponds noticeably to those which are made to Lancelot about the coming of Galahad. The grace of the Holy Ghost which had healed his love-madness sustains Lancelot during his month on the supernatural ship. The Holy Ghost 'in the lykenes of a fayre and a mervaylous flame' falls between Bors and Lionel to prevent fratricide. Above all it is associated with Galahad by ritual and symbol. It is significant that Galahad appears at court on the Feast of Pentecost which is not only the high point of the chivalric year but also the day when the Church celebrates the descent of the Holy Spirit.[18] The young knight is dressed in red armour and a coat of red sendal – the colour of Pentecostal flame. Later the flame symbol of the Holy Ghost will be combined with the image of the red rose,[19] as King Mordrains designates the nature of Galahad's power:

'. . . And thou arte the rose which ys the floure of all good vertu, and in colour of fyre. For the fyre of the Holy Goste ys takyn so in the that my fleyssh, whych was all dede of oldenes, ys becom agayne yonge'.

(1025)

In Christian iconography, the rose was a symbol of virginity associated both with Mary, the *Rosa caeli*, and with Christ. The analogy to the Holy Ghost is further suggested when Galahad is described as 'semely and demure as a dove'. The dove image, a traditional symbol of the Holy Ghost in Christian art since the sixth century,[20] is also associated with the Grail. Both Lancelot and Bors see a white dove bearing a golden censer when they are entertained at supernatural feasts in the Grail castle. The dove appears with the infant Galahad and the maiden carrying the Grail. The vessel is the means of stilling the terrible storm accompanying the adventures of the Perilous Bed. The white and gold of the image, as well as the sweet scent, the food-giving property, and the power over turbulent nature make it an apocalyptic symbol of considerable power. The author's development throughout *La Queste* of this image cluster – Holy Ghost, Galahad, fire, dove, and Grail – illustrates the manner in which the medieval mind used symbols to express something superhuman and only partly conceivable.

Below the Trinity in the celestial hierarchy are angels whose functions are to praise God, to act as his messengers, and to protect man against the devil.[21] Though the philosophers described them as pure minds unembodied, the artists gave them corporality *pro captu nostro*.[22] Both concepts are found in the *Morte Darthur*. Disembodied voices that explain, instruct, warn, and condemn are a favourite medium of allegory and prophecy. They also act as agents who control and direct the progress of the Grail knights in their quest. While praying in a ruined chapel, Galahad hears a voice that commands him to end the wicked customs of the Castle of Maidens. Lancelot is condemned for his sinfulness and ordered to leave holy places while Bors is directed to join Perceval at the seashore. On several occasions Malory increases the reliance on supernatural agency by attributing to celestial voices words that are spoken by human characters in *La Queste*; for example, after Galahad has released Earl Hernox from prison, a voice from on high commends him for taking vengeance on God's enemies and then instructs him to heal the Maimed King. One cannot always tell whether these voices are meant to be God Himself or God speaking through angels. Pseudo-Dionysus and Aquinas believed that God did nothing Himself that he could do through an intermediary but it is evidently God Himself who directs the Grail knights to leave Corbenic:

> 'My sunnes, and nat my chyeff sunnes, my frendis, and nat my werryours,
> go ye hens where ye hope beste to do, and as I bade you do'.
>
> (1031)[23]

Visible angels accompany Galahad on earth and bear his soul to heaven, performing a function often attributed to them in medieval art.[24] The soul of Lancelot, too, is heaved up to heaven by more angels than the number of men that the Archbishop has seen in one day. Angels anoint the Ship of Solomon and write prophetic letters. A great fellowship surrounds the Grail both at Corbenic and Sarras, combining the activities of protection, service, and adoration traditionally associated with them and illustrating the belief that angels are visible to men.

During the progress of the Grail quest, corporeal angels correspond to the enigmatic damsels, dwarfs, and magicians of secular romance who appear suddenly and disappear into thin air after initiating an adventure or rescuing a knight. Such an agent is the white knight who provides Galahad with his destined shield and recounts its history. His name cannot be revealed to Bagdemagus 'nother none erthely man'. Another celestial agent is the old man 'clothed in a surplyse in lyknes of a pryste' who stands at the helm of the white ship that saves Perceval from the wilderness. When questioned about his identity, he replies, 'Sir, I am of a strange contrey, and hydir I com to comforte you.' Lancelot too is visited by an old man who reprimands him for his wickedness and then vanishes so suddenly that the knight 'wyst not where he become'. Such hortatory and protective figures with supernatural powers influence the hero's progress in most quest myths.

In the great chain of being that linked all creatures to God, the good knights and hermits of Arthurian romance were only a little lower than the angels. The myth of class which is apparent in secular chivalric romance is adapted to the religious milieu by practically excluding the courtly ladies and by increasing the importance of the hermits. It is generally maintained that *La Queste del Saint Graal* was written to assert the superiority of *la chevalerie celestienne* and to denounce the vain endeavours of *la chevalerie terrienne*. However, Jean Frappier convincingly argues that the authors of the *Vulgate Prose Cycle* were condemning the errors of *chevalerie terrienne* but not the institution itself.[25] The knight alone represented for medieval man 'l'homme moderne, l'homme "réel", celui du milieu social alors vivant-et qui dans la perspective de l'oeuvre est la société prédestinée à qui est réservé de découvrir le secret du Graal.'[26] The belief that a knight was worthy to achieve the visions of mystic life through monastic virtue as well as to engage in active warfare had motivated St Bernard's sponsorship of the Templars, whose order combining chivalry and religion no doubt inspired the authors of *La Queste*.[27] In the *Prose Lancelot*, the Damsel of the Lake instructs the young hero at length on secular chivalric virtues which are, as Rosemond Tuve notes, almost the same as the Gifts of the Holy Ghost – *largesse*, *debonnairté*, *fortitude*, and *sagesse*.[28] Spiritual experience, then, was not to be reserved for the priesthood alone[29] but could be enjoyed by saintly knights and knightly hermits as well.

As in the secular myth, lineage is an important means of establishing the elite. The old man who presents Galahad to Arthur announces: 'Sir, I brynge you here a yonge knyght the whych ys of kynges lynage and of the kynrede of Joseph of Aramathy.' Guenevere confirms that Galahad's nobility is unquestioned:

> 'for he ys of all partyes comyn of the beste knyghtes of the worlde and of the hyghest lynage: for sir Launcelot ys com but of the eyghth degré from oure Lorde Jesu Cryst, and thys sir Galahad ys the nyneth degré from oure Lorde Jesu Cryst. Therefore I dare sey they be the grettist jantillmen of the worlde'.

> (865)

Most of this passage is original in Malory. The concept that the chosen knight is predestined by his genealogy is important also in Wolfram's *Parzival*, where considerable space is devoted to Perceval's family tree. In *Morte Darthur*, Perceval, King Pellenore's son, is designated as worthy by a miracle which occurs on the day when he is knighted by Arthur. A maiden of 'high blood' who had never spoken a word leads him to the Sege Perilous, announcing in a loud voice, 'Fair knyghte, take here thy sege, for that sege apperteyneth to the and to none other.' This incident does not occur in Malory's French source. The other Grail knights, Lancelot and Bors, trace their ancestry through their mother to King David, the ancestor also of Christ. Though the begetting of Galahad was in Vinaver's phrase 'an irretrievable offence against courtly love,'[30] it provided the necessary link between the Grail hero and the 'historical' tradition represented by the Tree of Jesse in Christian iconography.[31] Aristocratic privilege characterizes the monks and hermits, too. Almost without exception they are former knights, 'men of worship and prowesse' as

Malory describes them, using the values of secular chivalry. In the religious milieu they perform the function that Merlin had served in the early period of Arthur's kingship – elucidating puzzling events, advising the hero, controlling his actions, and making prophetic comments. The only representatives of the clergy to appear in the Grail romance, they are an elite who link the two chivalries.

In the mythic society of *La Queste* and *Morte Darthur*, courtly ladies are notable by their absence. At the initiation of the quest, the knights are warned by a messenger from the hermit Nacien

> that none in thys queste lede lady nother jantillwoman with hym, for hit ys nat to do in so hyghe a servyse as they laboure in. For I warne you playne, he that ys nat clene of hys synnes he shall nat se the mysteryes of oure Lorde Jesu Cryste.
>
> (869)

Only an occasional anchoress, Perceval's aunt, the Queen of the Waste Lands, and Perceval's saintly sister, a type of Virgin Mary, appear among the elect.[32]

A discussion of the vertical myth would not be complete without the fallen angels. Corresponding to the celestial hierarchy is a diabolical hierarchy, a feudal order of evil spirits warring against God on the battlefield of the world. Again, iconography is an important influence on the demonic images of romance. In early Christian art the devil appeared as a serpent, the tempter of Eve, and this remained a traditional symbol of the Middle Ages.[33] On Lancelot's first visit to Corbenic he kills a serpent in a tomb, 'an orryble and a fyendely dragon spyttyng wylde fyre oute of hys mowthe'. As a reward for delivering the people of Corbenic from the fiend, he is granted a sight of the dove and the Grail, symbols of divine grace. Bors also encounters a dragon at Corbenic. In this case, too, its destruction is followed by the appearance of the apocalyptic images. Perceval kills a serpent that is fighting with a young lion. Later the old man on the ship explains that 'the serpente betokenyth a fynde' and the lady who had upbraided him for killing her serpent is the devil himself.

In medieval literature and art the physical depiction of devils followed two modes. They might be presented with every attribute of grotesque horror, as they are in the Winchester Psalter's miniature of Hell Mouth or in the representations of the Last Judgment commonly found in cathedral art of the later Middle Ages. It is this kind of devil that Galahad banishes from the tomb in the churchyard. A hermit expels from the tomb of a pious monk a fiend so hideous 'that there was no man so hardeherted in the worlde but he sholde a bene aferde'. On the other hand, a devil might take the form of various terrestrial creatures. The great steed, blacker than any berry, that carries Perceval a four days' journey in less than an hour is a demonic creature. When the knight saves himself from destruction in the roaring water by making the sign of the cross, the devil's true nature is revealed, for 'he wente into the watir cryynge and rorynge and makying grete sorowe, and hit semed unto hym that the watir brente' (912). Frequently, medieval writers and preachers present the devil in the form of a seductive female who combines elements of the malevolent Celtic fées with those of the treacherous daughters of Eve denounced in patristic literature. Beauty, love, and all sensual delights are used to tempt the hero from the path of virtue. Bors is led to a castle, welcomed by knights and ladies, disarmed, decked out in a rich mantle furred with ermine, entertained with 'delytes and deyntees,' and offered the love of 'the rychyst lady and the fayryste of the worlde.' In secular terms, it is an ideal situation recalling the entertainment of a hero in the Otherworld castle of a fée. The beautiful lady uses all her wiles to tempt Bors' chastity, finally threatening to throw herself with her twelve attendants from a high battlement. Piously concluding that it is better for them to lose their souls than he his, Bors remains steadfast. The demonic origins of the tower and ladies are revealed when they disappear with a terrible noise and cry 'as all the fyndys of helle had bene aboute hym'.

The temptation of Perceval is conducted with a similar appeal to carnal desires. He has been abandoned in the heat of summer on a rocky shore with nothing to eat or drink. Suddenly a black ship travelling at supernatural speed brings him a beautiful lady dressed in rich clothes. After telling him a tale of woe allegorising the Fall of Lucifer (with whom this proud lady is to be identified) she orders her damsel to set up a pavilion on the gravel. After removing his armour, Perceval falls asleep in the shade. When he wakes, he finds that a marvellous feast has been spread with a great variety of meats and the strongest wine he has ever drunk. It is the fairy mistress theme adapted to moral allegory. Again, only the sign of the cross suggested by the sight of his sword's pommel saves the hero. The pavilion turns upside down and vanishes in smoke while the lady departs on her ship with the wind roaring about her and the water burning behind.

In addition to presenting the mythic agents as characters in a drama, the writers of romance also suggested their presence by means of symbols. Light and darkness, white and black, calm and storm are the anagogic symbols that usually represent the absolute antithesis of God and the devil.[34] Dante employed a well-established, universal image when he chose the life-giving, light-giving, heat-giving sun as the dominant symbol of the *Divine Comedy*. Dunbar explains its centrality: 'He who plunges at any point into the symbolism of the Middle Ages will find himself as it were in a solar vortex.'[35] Thirteenth-century aesthetic theory promoted a mystique of light, basing its idea of beauty on 'tout ce qui est clarté, lumière, splendeur'.[36]

The burning candle, the fiery sword, white and red, silver and gold are recurrent apocalyptic images in the Grail romance introduced to create a sense of beauty, of symbolic significances, and particularly of the magical colours in which, says de Bruyn, the Middle Ages delighted.[37] The burning candle represents Christ and the fiery sword God. Silver, symbolizing the wisdom of God and the humanity of Christ, and gold, symbolizing the brightness of God and royal power of Christ, convey through their refulgence an impression of transcendent reality. White signifies purity and divinity, red sacrifice and divine love; they are the colours of Christ and of Galahad whose armour and coat are red, whose white shield bears a red cross made with the blood of Josephé, and whose bright sword was drawn from a red stone.[38] One of the most ornately conceived artifacts is the sword which Galahad finds on the Ship of Solomon. The pommel is of multi-coloured stones, every colour with a different virtue. The handle is made from the ribs of a serpent and a fish with magical properties so that whoever possesses it will never be weary or hurt or distracted from whatever he sees before him. The image suggests Abbot Suger's description of the effect that contemplating precious and beautiful objects had on him:

> Thus, when – out of my delight in the beauty of the house of God – the loveliness of the many-coloured gems has called me away from external cares, and worthy meditation has induced me to reflect, transferring that which is material to that which is immaterial, on the diversity of the sacred virtues: then it seems to me that I see myself dwelling, as it were, in some strange region of the universe which neither exists entirely in the slime of the earth nor entirely in the purity of Heaven; and that, by the grace of God, I can be transported from this inferior to that higher world in an anagogical manner.[39]

In the same way, in *La Queste* and Malory, whenever there is a concentration of images associated with light, we understand an allusion to the spiritual world. Of course, it is sometimes difficult to distinguish the light-giving marvels of Christian myth from those of Celtic tradition for light was associated also with the pagan supernatural. For instance, the burning spear that threatens Bors in the Perilous Bed is a pagan weapon that has been assimilated into the spear of Longinus and the Spear of Vengeance.[40] At Corbenic it appears in the Grail procession flanked by children who carry light-giving tapers.

Light and a sweet scent are constantly associated with the Grail. From its chamber in Corbenic shines a 'grete lyght as hit were a somers lyght'. It is kept on an altar of silver over which hangs a silver sword so bright that it blinds Bors. When Lancelot makes his final visit to the Grail castle, he sees through the open door of the chamber 'a grete clerenesse, that the house was as bryght as all the tourcheis of the worlde had bene there'. When it goes abroad it glimmers in the forest and even though in its appearance at Arthur's court it is covered with white samite, nevertheless a sunbeam seven times brighter than any daylight shines on the knights.

Orthodox theology treated God's enemy negatively. Darkness was absence of light, evil absence of good. Yet the devil in popular sermon, legend, art and drama became an almost Manichean power who duplicated God's celestial society with demonic counterparts and who was generally depicted by means of sensory details arousing fear and horror.[41] Black smoke, burning heat, cacophony, tempest and evil smells indicated demonic presences, the association of fire and smoke being derived from Job 41:12–13: 'Out of his nostrils goeth smoke, like that of a pot heated and boiling. His breath kindleth coals and a flame cometh forth out of his mouth.' Perceval's demon horse and demon mistress vanish in fire and smoke, leaving a trail of burning water. The exorcised devil in the churchyard tomb is preceded by a foul smoke. The demon ship moves over the sea 'as all the wynde of the worlde had dryven hit', and the devil who recounts the miracle of the old monk disappears in a great tempest. Devils lurk in the darkness of tombs. They wear black armour and ride about on black horses or in ships hung with silk blacker than any berry. But although the visible world is an expression of the invisible, it is not always easy to distinguish the celestial from the demonic. Even the white-black antithesis is not foolproof, as Bors discovers when he sees in a vision a swan and a raven who demand that he choose between them. A man in religious 'weeds' (a demon in disguise) explains that the white bird is a beautiful lady who will die if her love is rejected. Later a *bona fide* abbot reveals the true significance of the images. The black bird is the Holy Church and the white bird the fiend, 'whyght withoutefurth and blacke within; hit ys ipocresye, which ys withoute yalew or pale, and semyth withouteforth the servauntis of Jesu Cryste, but they be withinfurthe so horrible of fylth and synne, and begyle the worlde so evyll' (967).

It seems that the enormous French Arthurian romance known as the *Vulgate Prose Cycle* was contrived to frame *La Queste del Saint Graal*. Having seduced their readers into a world containing the adventures of secular chivalry, the authors then used an apparently similar pattern of images in a continuous form to convey tropological and anagogical truths. Here again are quests and combats, feasting and tourneying, beautiful ladies and magic ships, but the *sens* is quite different in both *La Queste* and in Malory's adaptation *The Tale of the Sankgreal*[42] from the use of these motifs in the secular milieu. The Grail quest is not a nebulously ethical exhibition of chivalric prowess but an allegory of the soul's pilgrimage through life to eternity.[43] Its purpose is not the acquisition of 'much erthly worship' (Malory's phrase) though that too may come to the successful knight. It is the acquisition of divine grace and the enjoyment of the beatific vision that motivate the Grail Questers. That even the noblest of the Arthurian knights has jeopardised his soul by fighting for the wrong reasons is revealed to Lancelot by the voice of God:

'I have loste all that I have besette in the, for thou hast ruled the ayenste me as a warryoure and used wronge warris with vayneglory for the pleasure of the worlde more than to please me, therefore thou shalt be confounded withoute thou yelde me my tresoure'.

(928–929)

The significant passage from 'used' to 'me' is Malory's addition to his French source. The chief enemy of the Grail knight is not a giant, fay, or evil knight but the sins of lust, pride, avarice, self-indulgence, anger, and instability – the enemy within. When he resists the wiles of seductive damsels or refuses to joust against his brother, despite great provocation, or mortifies the flesh with a hair shirt and a diet of water and worts, the real victory is spiritual rather than material.

Like many Arthurian adventures the Grail Quest begins at the court of Arthur on the Feast of Pentecost, or more exactly, on the Vigil of the Feast when a maiden sent by King Pelles summons Lancelot to a nunnery in the forest. There he knights a young squire, Galahad, and returns directly to court by late morning. According to custom, Arthur and Guenevere with their nobles go first to services in the cathedral and then gather in the great hall. Rejoicing in the vitality of the Round Table, the King and Queen are passing glad at the return of Bors and Lionel and Lancelot 'hole and sounde' – so overjoyed, in fact, that Arthur forgets his 'olde custom' of refusing to begin the feast until he has seen some marvel (Malory's addition).

This is to be a Pentecostal Feast very different from those of secular romance. As had happened at the first meeting of the Round Table, magical letters of gold have appeared on the seats. On this day 'four hondred wynter and four and fyffty acomplyvysshed aftir the Passion of Oure Lorde Jesu Cryst' the Sege Perelous will be fulfilled. The verb indicates more than mere physical occupation. The appearance of Galahad will complete the Round Table; it will also precipitate the knights into a kind of experience unlike anything they have encountered before. The problem of the *geasa* is solved by the fortuitous appearance of Balin's sword floating down the river. It is fixed in the red stone of Merlin's making to await 'the beste knyght of the worlde'.[44] As often happens in secular romance, the arrival of a new knight precipitates a marvellous adventure. All the doors and windows of the palace shut automatically, as they had when Christ appeared to his disciples on Resurrection Sunday.[45] Galahad is presented to the court not by a relative or patron knight but by a celestial agent 'clothed all in whyght, and there was no knyght knew from whens he com'. The revelation of the new knight's lineage establishes his worthiness – but, again, it is a kind of worthiness not found in secular romance. Furthermore, the arming of this knight is only accomplished through the fulfilment of prophecy. His sword is a symbol of divinity, his shield a symbol of faith. Like all new knights he must prove his worth by engaging in a

4. *Galahad, Bors, Perceval and Perceval's sister sail towards the Ship of Solomon.*
Quête du Saint Graal (*London, British Library, MS.Royal 14 E III, f.125v.*)

tournament. For the first and last time Arthur will see the knights of the Round Table 'all hole togydirs'. Galahad is armed with a spear, a Crucifixion symbol that reminds us once more that he is a figuration of Christ. Only Lancelot and Perceval are not overthrown.

Throughout these introductory scenes it is evident that the author of *La Queste* is following the conventional chivalric pattern but each event is endowed with spiritual significance. Galahad's withdrawal of the sword in the stone establishes his superiority in the religious milieu as Balin's success had established him in the world of Celtic magic and Arthur's in the political sphere. Symbolic, also, are his filling of the Sege Perelous and of Arthur's bed. The significance of the former act is suggested by Charles Williams:

> The sitting of Galahad in the Siege is the condition precedent to all achievement; and Tennyson's phrase may serve for the moment – that he cried, 'If I lose myself I find myself.'[46]

By lying in Arthur's bed, Galahad shows that the spiritual takes precedence over the temporal. The Keeper of the Grail Castle long before had prophesied that the spiritual symbol would destroy the finest symbol of earthly power: '"When this thynge gothe abrode the Rounde Table shall be brokyn for a season"' (Malory's addition). Now 'there lies in the King's bed that which is the consummation and the destruction of the Table'.[47]

The Grail Quest is initiated not by the granting of a boon or the appearance of a magical emissary but by a mystical experience. As the court prepares to enjoy the customary feast after the tournament, the palace is shaken by a violent storm.

> Than anone they harde crakynge and cryynge of thundir, that hem thought the palyse sholde all to-dryve. So in the myddys of the blast entyrde a sonnebeame, more clerer by seven tymys than ever they saw day, and all they were alyghted of the grace of the Holy Goste. Than began every knyght to beholde other, and eyther saw other, by their semynge, fayrer than ever they were before. Natforthan there was no knyght that myght speke one worde a grete whyle, and so they loked every man on other as they had bene doome.
>
> Than entird into the halle the Holy Grayle coverde with whyght samyte, but there was none that myght se hit nother whom that bare hit. And there was all the halle fulfylled with good odoures, and every knyght had such metis and drynkes as he beste loved in thys worlde.
>
> (865)

The passage is worth quoting in full because it exemplifies Malory's ability to improve on his sources by adding vivid descriptive phrases. To the French author's skill is due the felicitous combination of a chivalric feast, the Biblical account of the first Pentecost in Acts 2, 1–4, and the sensory expressions of medieval mysticism. As a result of the Grail's presence, the very appearance of the knights changes 'and eyther saw other, by their semynge, fayrer than ever they were before'. One knows that the illumination is not only external, that the meat and drink are not merely material. The desire and fulfilment that mark a Christian's relations with God are symbolized in this Pentecostal feast provided by the Grail.

It would seem that the mystical experience might have ended at Arthur's court. Since the Grail has already appeared to all the knights at the centre, why ride off into the Waste Forest to seek it? The answer is that the Grail has not appeared openly, its full meaning has not been understood. It is covered in white samite to protect it from the eyes of the world. Gawain makes a vow that is taken up by all the knights:

> I shall laboure in the queste of the Sankgreall, and . . . I shall holde me oute a twelve-month and a day or more if nede be, and never shall I returne unto the courte agayne tylle I have sene hit more opynly than hit hath bene shewed here.
>
> (866)

The vow and the time-span allotted for the quest are conventional; Arthur's despair at the departure of the knights is not. From secular quests they returned triumphantly; from this many will not return and of those who do, only one will have succeeded. Ironically, it is Lancelot who applies the worldly standard: 'A, sir, . . . comforte yourself! For hit shall be unto us a grete honoure. . . .'

The knights of secular romance rode 'by chance', accepting any adventure they encountered though they seldom knew where it would end. They moved in a cycle of time and place unrelated to historical reality. The Grail knights, on the contrary, move in the stream of historical time (their quest takes place four hundred and fifty-four years after the Crucifixion) and make for a particular place, the castle of Corbenic. Yet their journey is essentially psychological, though it is projected into an external landscape. Setting out from Camelot after the appearance of the Grail, they ride together to the castle of Vagon; 'than every knyght toke the way that hym lyked beste'. The difficulties of the spiritual life are symbolized by the hostile landscapes through which the heroes must pass. Wild and strange are the waste forests, steep mountains, dark valleys, desert islands, rocky shores, and tumultuous rivers. Supernatural ships are driven by tempests along barren coasts. Images of desolation and abandonment reflect the verses of the Psalmist. The wilderness landscape is that of Jeremiah, the wandering children of Israel, Christ, and John the Baptist. Pauphilet suggests that the trees of the Waste Forest signify evil desires, adding, 'Comme le désert, la forêt est un lieu sans resources, lieu d'erreurs, lieu de mort.'[48] Ferdinand Lot describes the landscape of the *Lancelot* as a marvellous garden of love; in comparison, the *Quête du Graal* presents 'un désert aride: rien qu'un grand ciel brûlant au-dessus d'une terre morte, où ne s'epanouissent ni le parfum des fleurs, ni le chant des oiseaux'.[49]

In the romantic forest no knight-errant was ever at a loss for a guide and he seldom travelled far without meeting another knight. In this forest only the chosen few receive direction or encounter testing adventures. Instead of proceeding companionably together, they usually travel alone, each seeking salvation in his own way. Galahad rides far ahead, appearing only when Perceval, Bors, or Lancelot needs help and comfort. The worldly knights wander vainly through trackless wastes. Gawain's fate is typical:

> . . . he rode longe withoute ony adventure, for he founde nat the tenthe parte of aventures as they were wonte to have. For sir Gawayne rode frome Whytsontyde tylle Mychaellmasse, and founde never adventure that pleased hym.
>
> (941)

Even when he is told the way that Galahad has taken, he is unable to follow and though he had found Corbenic in the secular milieu, its location now eludes him. Finding the right way is more than a matter of geography since the conventions of secular romance no longer apply. When Melias with the bravado of terrestrial chivalry ignores the cross's warning against taking the left hand way, he nearly loses his life. A monk explains that 'the way on the ryght hande betokenyd the hygheway of oure Lorde Jesu Cryst, and the way of a good trew lyver. And the other way betokenyth the way of synnars and myssebelevers' (886). Furthermore, the hospitable castles, manor houses, and pavilions that were so prominent a feature of the secular world are difficult and dangerous to find. No longer do welcoming lords, beautiful ladies, silken pavilions and delicious food and drink appear as rewards for prowess. On the contrary, they are the devil's lures. Even the wells and fountains become allegorical images. In Ector's vision, Lancelot is unable to drink from a fair well representing the grace of God and must go away thirsty. In contrast, the boiling well in the perilous forest, 'a sygne of lechory that was that tyme muche used' (the temporal allusion is Malory's), is instantly cooled by Galahad's virginity.

Hermitages, abbeys of white monks, and ruined chapels are particularly associated with the allegorical landscape since they often provide occasions for instruction. At a white abbey near Camelot Galahad acquires the shield of King Evelake which has been preserved there for the destined knight. At white abbeys Bors learns the significance of his adventures, Lancelot finds the tomb of King Bagdemagus, and the Maimed King waits for Galahad. After he has been healed, he yields himself 'to a place of religion of whyght monkes'. These abbeys are not only shelters for the Grail knights but also repositories of the Grail tradition. Their place in the landscape may be due to Cistercian authorship.[50] Chapels are common enough scenes of stasis along the adventurous way, where corpses may be laid, or a knight might be healed or judged or allowed privacy to bare his soul. In the country of the Grail, however, there is a discrepancy between the decayed exteriors in their wild setting and the marvellously preserved interiors with rich artefacts, mystical visions and other-world voices. Riding through a wild and pathless forest, Lancelot comes to a stone cross by an old chapel. Inside he sees a fair altar richly arrayed with a silken cloth, and a silver candelabrum with six great candles. Although the chapel door is 'waste and brokyn' he can find no place to enter. While he sleeps on his shield beside the cross, the altar and candelabrum leave the chapel without human agency and join the Grail to heal a sick knight. It is Lancelot's sin that deprives him of power to go where he likes and that keeps him mute and helpless in the presence of the Grail. His failure in his adventure contrasts sharply with his success in entering the Perilous Chapel of secular romance. At another ancient wasted chapel Gawain and Ector see strange visions and hear disembodied voices that reveal the inadequacies of worldly knights. Unlike Lancelot, they refuse to profit from their instruction.

Even the knight's relationship to his horse takes on a new meaning. In secular romance the loss of a mount was an accident soon mended by prowess, command, or courtesy, but in the Grail quest it becomes a moral test or spiritual symptom. When Perceval loses first his horse and then a borrowed palfrey, he accepts from a devil woman a demon horse that attempts to carry him to hell. Only the sign of the cross saves him. The knight healed by the Grail takes Lancelot's helm, sword and steed while the hero sleeps, numbed by the 'dedly synne whereof he was never confessed'. Realising that without his helmet, sword, and horse he cannot achieve adventures, he sets out on foot until he reaches a hermitage. When he has repented, confessed, forsworn the queen's company and done penance, he is promised the restoration of his horse and arms. Ector's vision of Sir Lancelot falling from his horse and riding on an ass signifies this newfound penitence and humility. Knights who are in a state of grace have no difficulty finding horses. When the Grail heroes board the Ship of Solomon, they take their saddles and bridles but leave their horses behind. Landing near the castle of Cartelois in the marches of Scotland, they seize the horses of their attackers 'for they had no horse in that contrey, for they lefft their horsys whan they toke their shippe'. The explanation is Malory's – another example of his realistic approach to horses. When Galahad concludes his journey on the barge of Perceval's sister, a white knight (that is, a divine agent) presents him with a white horse on which to ride to Corbenic. The colour is appropriate both to a hero and a virgin.

In the religious allegory, arms and armour have a theological significance based on St Paul's letter to the Ephesians:

> Let Christ Jesus himself be the armour that you wear. Put on all the armour which God provides, so that you may be able to stand firm against the devices of the devil. . . . Buckle on the belt of truth; for coat of mail put on integrity; let the shoes on your feet be the gospel of peace, to give you firm footing; and, with all these, take up the great shield of faith, with which you will be able to quench all the flaming arrows of the evil one. Take salvation for helmet; for sword, take that which the Spirit gives you, – the words that come from God.[51]

The monks and hermits are knights who have clothed themselves 'in a relygious wede and in the armour of oure Lorde'. Bors puts off his secular armour and wears a scarlet coat symbolizing penance, faith, and a rejection of violence. Galahad's swords, as we have seen, signify his Messianic role while his red armour further develops his figuration of Christ. Perceval is saved from the devil by the sight of his sword with its cross-shaped pommel while Lancelot's reliance on his secular sword rather than on the sword of faith marks him as one who cannot reject the values of *la chevalerie terrienne* even at the threshold of Corbenic. But when he has atoned for his twenty-four years of sin in a penitential swoon, he is clothed in a robe of scarlet, fresh and new, as a symbol of his new spiritual state. The broken sword in the Grail castle[52] is a folkloric weapon which has been given a Christian history. Originally the creative symbol of a vegetation myth, it is now the weapon that smote Josephé when he endeavoured to convert a heathen king. The failure of Bors and Perceval to mend the sword and Galahad's subsequent success confirm the latter's position as the paramount Grail hero.

Isolated from the everyday world and from human contact, his apprehensions sharpened by fasts and prayers, the Grail knight perceives with unusual clarity and freshness. Whether waking or sleeping, he has splendid visions of the beauty touched with strangeness that for Pater was the essence of romance and for the medieval mystics was the attribute of divinity. No other books of *Morte Darthur* are so aesthetically rich as the pageant of the Grail. The imagery of the visions is generally Scriptural and patristic yet Celtic magic must have contributed touches of the marvellous. Since it was believed in the Middle Ages that dreams might be divinely inspired to reveal the future or impart knowledge,[53] these visions of romance and religion are patently didactic.

The allegorical landscape through which the knights travel gives continuity to the quest. In contrast, the allegorical images in the landscape of the human mind produce a sense of isolation and individuality. Each knight's visions are fitted to his particular spiritual state. Lancelot's sinfulness is symbolised by stone, bitter wood, and a barren fig tree but because he is not hopelessly lost, he sometimes sees angels. Gawain, who typifies the worldly knights of the Round Table, sees a fertile meadow filled with proud black bulls that go to seek better pasture and return so thin they cannot stand. Bors, who strives with conscious effort to attain grace, dreams of confusing choices to be made between a swan and a raven, a lily and a rotten tree. Perceval, the naive man who is saved by inherent grace, dreams of ladies and beasts that symbolise the Old Law of the devil and the New Law of Christ. Galahad alone enjoys the full mystical vision of 'the spirituall thyngcs'. By means of visions the concrete, historical and personal are brought into contact with the abstract, timeless and universal so that the cycle of waking and dreaming life experienced by the questers is both realistic and transcendent.

Battles in the religious milieu are spiritual conflicts undertaken to assert moral principles but not to inflict death. Homicide was condemned by the authors of *La Queste*, except when the enemies were pagans. Following Prudentius, the opposition of good and evil had been expressed in literature, art, and sermon through the *psychomachia*, often presented in the form of a battle between good and evil knights for possession of a castle.[54] The Castle of Maidens adventure in the *Morte Darthur* belongs to this tradition. In the secular romance, this castle on the Severn had been the scene of a great tournament where Tristram had won renown. It is now 'a cursed castle . . . for all pité ys oute thereoff, and all hardynes and myschyff ys therein'. Ignoring the conventional warning, Galahad attacks and defeats the castle's defenders, seven brothers who represent the Seven Deadly Sins.[55] The delivery of the castle becomes an allegory of the Harrowing of Hell[56] for when Galahad opens the gates, he is greeted by a great crowd of people crying, 'Sir, ye be wellcom, for longe have we abydyn here oure delyveraunce!' Galahad does not kill the evil brothers. Murder is left to the worldly knights, Gawain, Gareth and Iwain. The Grail knight's participation in this event illustrates St Bernard's dictum that the practice of good works should precede the holy quiet of contemplation, as the blossom precedes the fruit. The tournament of black and white knights in which Lancelot engages is another *psychomachia*. Following the ritual of *la chevalerie terrienne*, he joins the black knights, the weaker party, in order to increase his 'shevalry'. For the first time in his life he suffers a humiliating defeat. More clearly than any homily this event makes him realize that in the religious quest there is a relationship between success and one's spiritual condition: '. . . And now I am shamed, and am sure that I am more synfuller than ever I was.' The significance of the tournament is explained by a recluse:

'A, Launcelot,' seyde she, 'as longe as ye were knyght of erthly knyght-hode ye were the moste mervayloust man of the worlde, and most adventurest. 'Now,' seyde the lady, 'sitthen ye be sette amonge the knyghtis of hevynly adventures, if adventure falle you contrary at that

turnamente yet have ye no mervayle; for that turnamente yestirday was
but a tokenynge of oure Lorde . . . the erthely knyghtes were they which
were clothed all in blake, and the coveryng betokenyth the synnes whereof
they be nat confessed. And they with the coverynge of whyght betokenyth
virginité, and they that hath chosyn chastité.

(933)

Not only were the white knights sustained by their virginity but, Malory adds,
they were also assisted by the appearance of the Grail (a source of grace). Again
the adventure at the Castle of Corteloise with its dispossessed lord, ravished
maiden, evil defenders and Arthurian avengers seems to follow the conventional pattern of secular romance. By killing a great number of the people who
are fighting against them, the heroes restore political and social order. Yet this,
too, is a *psychomachia* in which the virtuous Grail knights defeat the vicious
pagans. The violence is approved by a priest and a celestial voice affirms that
the questers have been engaged on God's behalf against the devil's forces.

Malory's treatment of the two chivalries differs from his source in the
emphasis that he puts on virtuous character rather than on religious dogma as a
means of attaining grace.[57] In Malory's view, it is a virtuous character that
ensures success in both the terrestrial and the celestial sphere. For personal as
well as aesthetic reasons, he greatly reduces the homiletic content of his source.
At the same time, he attributes failure in the Grail quest to weakness of
character rather than to theological aberrations.[58] While Lancelot's virtue in
the chivalric milieu is underlined by the addition of several original passages,[59]
his failure in the religious milieu is attributed to the moral faults of pride,
sensuality and instability, faults revealed by his reaction to aspects of the
environment. The French Lancelot attempts to close his mind to the material
world and gain mystical union with God. The sights and sounds of the spring
morning with its shining sun (a divine symbol) and its singing birds only
increase his sense of shame. Malory's Lancelot, on the other hand, is com-
forted by the birds singing at dawn after his disastrous experience at the
Perilous Chapel and a month at sea makes him glad 'to play hym by the watirs
syde, for he was somewhat wery of the shippe'. Even after his penance and
asceticism have brought him to Corbenic, he still reacts to danger as a worldly
knight and draws his sword against the lions instead of trusting in God. His
behaviour provides a contrast to that of Perceval who had helped a lion (Christ)
against a serpent (the Devil) with the result that 'the lyon wente allwey aboute
hym fawnynge as a spaynell' (Malory's simile). Perceval rejoices in the animal's
company and thanks God for it.[60]

While the treatment of the two chivalries involves moral allegory (tropolo-
gy), the treatment of Scripture is typological and anagogic. It provides another
kind of patterning, one that utilizes movement in the stream of time rather than
a *psychomachia*. The basis of typology in *La Queste* is the progress from the Old

Law to the New.[61] As we have already seen, Galahad is presented as a Christ-figure who exorcises devils, frees souls from bondage, heals the sick and blind, and revives the Waste Land. He represents the New Law which has delivered God's people and revealed divine truth. The tension between the two laws is introduced at several points. The white knight tells Galahad that King Evelake had been saved from defeat and death by his conversion to the new way, symbolised by the image of the Crucified Christ on his shield. Perceval's dream of the serpent ridden by an old lady and the lion ridden by a young one is an allegory not only of the enmity between the Devil, represented by the serpent, and Christ, represented by the lion, but also of that between Synagogue who nourished the Devil and Holy Church, born from the Crucifixion and Resurrection of Christ, and representing 'fayth, good hope, belyeve and baptyme'.[62] When Bors abandons his brother Lionel in order to help the kidnapped damsel, he is aiding 'the newe law of oure Lord Jesu Cryst and Holy Chirche' while his rejection of the beautiful temptress foils 'the olde lawe and the fynde which all day warryth agenst Holy Chirch'.

Other characters in the romance may be regarded as types of Biblical characters. Locke interprets Guenevere and the Queen of the Waste Lands as Eve-types while Perceval's sister represents the Virgin Mary.[63] Hennessy compares Lancelot with Solomon, Samson and Absolom while Perceval is a new Jonas and Daniel. She further suggests that typology affects the structure of romance through 'the sense it gives of perpetual recurrence, of an endless repetition of an eternally ordained pattern'.[64] Wallace Stevens' comment on echo technique may well be applied to the fine web of inter-related images and concepts in the allegorical Grail Quest: 'It is not too extravagant to think of resemblances and of the repetitions of resemblances as a source of the ideal.'[65]

Because the section entitled by Vinaver 'Sir Galahad' does little to carry forward the story line, the modern reader may pass over it quickly and uncomprehendingly. Yet the Ship of Solomon image provides a good example of that order imposed by correspondences that appealed particularly to the medieval mind. In recounting to the Grail knights the history of the ship and its artifacts, Perceval's sister links contemporary history (the Grail quest) to universal history conceived as a continuous uninterrupted progress from the Creation to the Last Judgment.[66] The mystic vision which Galahad achieves at Sarras climaxes a train of events that began with the Fall. Solomon's Ship provides the necessary transition. Many intervening events, some Biblical, some pseudo-historical, are recalled in the account – the murder of Abel (an innocent victim like Christ), the reign of Solomon (a representation of peace), the Passion of Christ, the coming of Grail and lance to Logres, and the wasting of the land which still awaits deliverance. Like the fairy ships of Celtic romance, this vessel is free from the temporal and spatial limitations of the real world. A sacred place which isolates the Grail knights and allows them to concentrate on spiritual matters, it is described as the Ship of Faith[67] which can be boarded only by those 'in stedefaste beleve'. And it is a treasure-house of symbolic artifacts. There is the blood-red sword of David destined for Galahad as token of his lineage and election. There are three spindles made from the Tree of Life[68] – one white as snow, a symbol of paradisal purity, one green as grass, a symbol of procreation, one red as blood, a symbol of violence. There is a rich bed[69] in which the last knight of Solomon's kindred shall rest, and the sword's wonderful girdle (representing the New Testament), made from the hair of Perceval's sister to replace the hempen girdle of the Old Testament. Locke aptly defines the Ship of Solomon as 'the ingathering of the images'.

The Grail quest proceeds from Camelot (the familiar world) through wastes and over waters to Corbenic and, finally, to Sarras. The knight's progress is impeded by settings and situations which test his moral and spiritual worth. In spite of the fact that the *rite de passage* appears to be taking place in a physically apprehensible landscape, the true direction of the mystical quest is inward and private. The Round Table set in a meadow of humility and patience fails because its knights – all but three – 'turned into waste contreyes: that signifieth dethe' instead of seeking the centre with patience and humility.

The Grail Castle Corbenic[70] is a place of mystery, and to some extent, of inconsistency. When first encountered in *The Tale of Balin*, its invisible knight and vengeful lord make it seem a demonic setting. Balin's wild chase through endless rooms, his striking of the Dolorous Blow, the shattering of the castle and the wasting of three kingdoms are events in a nightmare. In contrast, the description of Lancelot's first visit evokes the image of a real medieval town with its bridge, castle, tower and crowd of villagers. The impression is reinforced when Lancelot returns in his madness to be stoned and beaten by the village boys, bedded on straw under the castle gate, and thrown meat from a distance because he is regarded as dangerous. And, since he is a part of castle life, he is decked in a scarlet robe to celebrate the knighting of Pelles' nephew. The Corbenic which Bors visits seems a different kind of place again. It combines domesticity (Elaine with her child in her arms) and mysticism (the Grail procession) with the perilous adventures of an Otherworld fortress[71] and the visionary allegories that prophesy historical events. Directed by his aunt, Perceval visits Corbenic, looking for Galahad, and finds it to be 'an house closed well with wallys and depe dyches'.

While Camelot is specifically identified with Winchester, the geographic location of Corbenic is not made clear. It may not even be in Logres, for King Pelles introduces himself as 'kynge of the forayne contré'. It is part of its mystery that, like the Grail itself, it seems almost to move about, as elusive as the spiritual state it represents. In the early visits of Bors and Lancelot, Corbenic seems not far from Camelot. When Elaine leaves Arthur's court, the king and a hundred knights bring her on her way through a forest, as if her home were located just on the other side. Yet the Grail knights traverse endless forests and wastelands and are borne far across the sea before they reach their destination. A sense of slowly passing time and of almost limitless space is conveyed by the description of Lancelot's journey on the ship with his son:

> So dwelled sir Launcelot and Galahad within that shippe halff a yere and served God dayly and nyghtly with all their power. And often they aryved in yles ferre frome folke, where there repayred none but wylde beestes, and ther they founde many straunge adventures and peryllous which they brought to an end.
>
> (1013)

Lancelot's final visit to Corbenic adds several details to one's conception of the castle. After a month's journey over the sea, the marvellous ship carrying Perceval's dead sister brings the quester at midnight[72] to a castle 'on the backe syde whiche was rych and fayre' (1014).[73] Bright moonlight reveals on the seaward side an open gate guarded by lions. Though sometimes a symbol of Christ, the animals here may signify the devil who 'walketh about as a roaring lion seeking whom he may devour.'[74] Directed by a celestial voice, Lancelot leaves the ship and safely passes the lions by making the sign of the cross,[75] though he had at first tried to protect himself with his sword. He crosses the courtyard and enters the keep where everyone is asleep. From room to room he passes, finding every door open until he reaches one that cannot be forced and beyond it he hears 'a voice whych sange so swetly that hit semede none erthely thynge'.

Essentially, Corbenic exists to enshrine the Grail and to permit the observances appropriate to it. Loomis believes that the Grail castle retains five traces of the old pagan traditions about the entertainment of a hero in the mansion of a god:

> the setting is not a chapel but a castle hall; there is the bleeding spear, recalling the spear of Lugh; there is the dish which provides the food one most desires; the castle is named Corbenic, which can most plausibly be explained as a corruption of *corbenoit*, 'blessed horn,' that is, the magic drinking horn of Bran; there is the Maimed King, whose prototype was the wounded Bran.[76]

Into this pagan setting the authors of *La Queste* introduced a celebration of the Christian mass which combined three contemporary theological concepts – the Divine Liturgy, the Apostolic Communion, and the miracle of Transubstantiation. Naturally, they minimised the importance of the pagan motifs – the asking of the question, the mending of the sword, and the healing of king and kingdom.

The Grail chamber is a richly furnished Christian shrine containing a silver altar, a chalice covered with red samite, brightly burning candles, a cross and other sacramental objects. It has, however, many unusual attributes. It is filled with angelic presences, disembodied voices, unearthly music, supernatural light.[77] A *geasa* forbids the entry of all but the elect when a mass is being celebrated. Because Lancelot disregards the warning and hurries forward to assist the priest, he is struck down by a fiery breath. Sometimes it seems not a chapel but a castle hall in the midst of which there is set the bed of the Maimed King. This is where Pelles had entertained Lancelot on his first visit and again on his recovery from his swoon. The Grail provides 'all manner of meates and drynkes' that they desire[78] and the Grail procession always forms part of the ceremonies, the holy vessel still carried by a woman, as it had been in the earliest versions.[79] In its final appearance at Corbenic there is a procession of angels, two bearing candles of wax, a third with a towel, a fourth with the bleeding spear. Bors had seen the dove and the golden Grail, Balin a golden bed and the marvellous spear on a table of gold with silver legs, Perceval the bed of the Maimed King and the altar which found its way to the Ship of Solomon. None of these knights had found difficulty in entering Corbenic. Yet when Ector bangs on the front door and shouts 'Undo!' the King comes to the window and warns him away, because he is 'one of them whych have servyd the fyende, and haste leffte the servyse of oure Lorde'.

The inconsistencies matter not at all, for the Grail Castle's nature is determined by the needs and deserts of each who finds it. Whether the refreshment is physical or spiritual, the imagery is richly sensuous and supernaturally suggestive. Lancelot must endure the lions and the fiery breath, yet is rewarded by a partial vision, a scarlet robe and a feast provided by the Grail. The 'verrey knights' see the image of Christ Himself and are fed with 'swete metis that never knyghtes yet tasted'.

The magical food-producing dish of Celtic myth, the platter of the Paschal Lamb, the chalice of the Last Supper, the Vessel in which Joseph of Arimathea caught Christ's blood and the luminous source of healing power become in *La Queste* and in the *Morte Darthur* primarily a symbol of grace. Gilson defines the controlling ideal as 'la vie de Dieu dans l'âme par sa charité, qui est la grâce'.[80] The words of a modern Catholic philosopher illuminate the concept of the two chivalries by which the Vulgate authors presented the theology, a concept concretely signified by the castles of Camelot and Corbenic:

> Mystical language knows only two terms, life according to the sense and life according to the spirit; those who sleep in their senses are those who wake in the Holy Spirit. . . . Man has a spiritual soul, but which informs a body. If it be a question of passing to a life wholly spiritual, his reason does not suffice; his tentatives toward angelism always fail. His only authentic spirituality is bound to grace and to the Holy Spirit.[81]

It is grace that gives man the power he has lost in the fall by restoring to him free will:

> Libera voluntas nos facit nostros; mala diaboli; bona, Dei. . . . Sane diabolo nostra nos mancipate voluntas, non ipsius potestas: Deo subjicit ejus gratia, non nostra voluntas.[82]

The secular knight reacts conventionally and even thoughtlessly to stereotyped situations. The Grail knight must make choices and seek to distinguish the divine will from the phantasmagoria of appearance.

As Gilson notes, the properties of the Grail are those which the Cistercians associated with grace. It appears at Pentecost in conditions which suggest the descent of the Holy Spirit on the apostles. It covers the table with food and drink suited to each taste. It sustains the sick and wounded. Its attributes appeal primarily to the senses – bright light, sweet scent, gold and samite, delicious flavours – for the Augustinian mystics described the beatific vision in sensuous rather than intellectual terms. The heightened aestheticism of the Grail book in comparison with other tales of the *Morte Darthur* can be attributed to the two-fold influence of mystical theology and the iconography of religious art. But the images of delight are those associated also with secular and pagan castles.

The Grail quest is not completed at Corbenic. Despite the achievement of the Grail by Arthurian knights, Logres is doomed. The Grail must be taken out of Arthur's kingdom because, as Christ announces, when He comes out of the Grail with the signs of the Passion upon His body:

> he ys nat served nother worshipped to hys ryght by hem of thys londe, for they be turned to evyll lyvyng, and therefore I shall disherite them of the honoure whych I have done them.

(1030)

The questers must journey on with the Hallows until they reach Sarras where Galahad will enjoy a mystical vision more complete than that of Corbenic. Historically, Sarras is Jerusalem, the centre of the medieval world, won from the pagans by Crusaders and provided with a Christian ruler. Symbolically, it is the New Jerusalem through which Galahad passes on his way to the City of God. The events in Sarras confirm what has already been suggested: namely, that the Grail quest is ultimately not horizontal but vertical. Vertical movement has been evident throughout the tale. From the subterranean world of hell devils rise to infest tombs or to tempt knights on the battlefield of the world. Re-enacting the Harrowing of Hell, Galahad descends into a cave that flames like the fiery pit. Angels descend from the celestial regions to the sub-lunar world, the Three Persons of the Trinity are present among men, and the Grail castle has the symbolic significance of a sacred mountain joining heaven and earth. If God is to triumph, man's final journey must be heavenward. For this reason the symbolic objects of the quest and the quester himself are borne up to heaven by a divine hand and a multitude of angels.

Unlike the secular quests from which heroes return to court victorious, the Grail quest defeats all but the chosen few. This failure is symptomatic of those to come. The ordered and harmonious society established by the Round Table is no longer secure, as Galahad's parting message for Lancelot indicates, '. . . bydde hym remembir of this worlde unstable' (1035, Malory's addition). Bors' report to the court contains an irony uncharacteristic of these occasions in the past. A pervasive note of sadness underlies the 'grete joy' traditionally felt by the court 'of the remenaunte that were com home'.

5

The Colde Erthe

Returning to the secular world after the conclusion of 'The Tale of the Sankgreal', Malory creates two original episodes, 'The Great Tournament' and 'The Healing of Sir Urry', to glorify Arthurian society; and he describes courtly rituals with a greater attention to detail than he has ever attempted before. But the society which on the surface seems so glamorous and glorious is fundamentally changed. The virtues of fellowship, loyalty, compassion, and service no longer unify the Knights of the Round Table. The courtly love that had earlier inspired knightly prowess becomes destructive and dishonourable. The ideal of kingship is also affected as Arthur's role changes from that of heroic conqueror and generous, hospitable lord to ruthless judge and publicly acknowledged cuckold.[1] The diminution of courtly values may be observed by examining five ceremonial occasions that apparently exalt the greatest society in the world but that actually reveal its fallibility – Guenevere's feast, the tournament at Camelot, the Great Tournament, Guenevere's maying party, and the return of Guenevere to Arthur at the Pope's command. Having fallen out with Lancelot because of his service to 'ladyes, madyns and jantillwomen',[2] (a service that was an essential part of his chivalric oath), the Queen invites twenty-four knights to a private dinner in London. She is motivated as much by spite against Lancelot as by a desire to honour other knights in a courtly way. As usual, Malory dignifies the occasion not by describing the feast but by providing a catalogue of participants that concludes with yet another reference to the treasonable murder of Lamerok by Gawain and his brothers. However, one dish is mentioned because it is essential to the plot. To please Gawain 'all maner of fruyte' is provided, including apples that have been poisoned by Lamerok's cousin Sir Pynell in the expectation that they will be eaten by Gawain. Instead, it is an Irish knight, Sir Patryse, who falls victim, and Guenevere is charged with his murder. The episode is significant not only because it reveals the continuing weakening of the Round Table by the Lot-Pellinore feud but also because it reveals a diminishment of the court's loyalty to Guenevere, and, by implication, to the king. Though Arthur reminds the knights of the universal shame that will result if the queen is burnt at the stake for want of a defender and though Bors reminds them of the generosity that she has always shown them, the court's willingness to believe the worst and unwillingness to act on the queen's behalf show a singular lack of courtesy.

'The Fair Maid of Astolat' which follows 'The Poisoned Apple' continues the theme of courtly inadequacy. For the first time, Lancelot appears at a tournament wearing a lady's token, a sleeve of scarlet embroidered with pearls, the gift of Elaine of Astolat. The courtliness of the gesture is superficial rather than substantial for he is motivated only by his desire to hide his identity. In the ideal world of knight-errantry, for example, in 'The Tale of Sir Gareth' or 'The Book of Sir Tristram', a hero's use of disguise adds to the jollity but here it has tragic consequences. Because she is already passionately in love, Elaine takes seriously his joking remark, 'ye may sey that I do more for youre love than ever y ded for lady or jantillwoman' (1068) and interprets his wearing of her sleeve as a sign of devotion (as does Guenevere when she learns of it). For Elaine, Lancelot becomes the armed knight at the lady's feet. She is not misleading Gawain in assuring him, 'Sertaynly, sir, . . . he ys my love', though she later admits that that is not the same as being his love. Lancelot refuses to have her either as wife – 'I never applyed me yett to be maryed' – or paramour – 'For than I rewarded youre fadir and youre brothir full evyll for their grete goodnesse.' To Elaine's pleading – 'fayre knyght and curtoyse knyght have mercy uppon me, and suffir me not to dye for youre love' – he can conceive of no better response than the offer of a thousand pound annuity to any good knight who will marry her. The beautiful corpse laid in the black barge and covered to the waist in cloth of gold moves the king, queen and all the knights to tears when it is brought down the Thames to Westminster. 'Sir,' says the queen to Lancelot, 'ye myght have shewed hir som bownte and jantilnes whych myght have preserved hir lyff.' But in this adventure the hero's courtesy has been limited by his loyalty to the queen.

The Great Tournament is held at Westminster on Candlemas day (February 2nd). It seems to be a return to the golden age of chivalry. The knights are glad when it is announced and make themselves ready 'in the freysshyste manner'. The days of jousting are followed by great feasts, revels, games, plays, and 'he that was curteyse, trew, and faythefull to hys frynde was that tyme cherysshed'. However, on this occasion, as at the Winchester tournament, Lancelot fights against the king, foreshadowing the more serious opposition to come.

'The Knight of the Cart' begins with a conventional, but for Malory uncharacteristic, analogy between the worlds of man and nature. The association of love and spring and love and Guenevere (who, we are told, had a good end because she was a true lover) leads naturally enough to Guenevere's desire 'to ryde on-maynge into woodis and fyldis besydes Westemynster' where the burgeoning and flourishing trees and herbs might be expected to renew a man

5. Arthur and Mordred meet in the last battle. St Albans Chronicle (*London, Lambeth Palace Library, MS.6, f.66v.*)

and woman and give all lovers 'corrayge' (the root of this virtue is *cor*-heart). The cavalcade is symmetrically balanced as ten Round Table knights, named in a catalogue, are paired with ten ladies and supported by ten squires and twenty yeomen. In a digression that suggests a renewal of chivalry, Malory tells us about the Queen's Knights, young candidates for membership in the Order of the Round Table, lacking heraldic designations but always carrying in battles, tournaments and jousts plain white shields. The pageantic aspect of the May Day entertainment is emphasised by references to the colours and the materials of the costumes. Guenevere instructs that 'ye all be clothed all in gryne, othir in sylke othir in clothe'. Green, of course, is the colour of spring. In medieval colour symbolism it also denoted love[3] and there was a further association with fées,[4] reminding us that the archetype of the kidnapping episode seems to have been a Celtic tale in which the abducted lady is a fée who has taken a mortal husband.[5] Decorating the green costumes of the knights are herbs, mosses and fresh flowers. Guenevere's happy excursion is rudely terminated:

> so there cam oute of a wood sir Mellyagaunte with an eyght score men, all harneyst as they shulde fyghte in a batayle of areste, and bade the quene and her knyghtis abyde, for magré their hedis they shulde abyde.
>
> (1122)

The Queen and her company are kidnapped by a Knight of the Round Table who is an unsatisfied courtly lover. By the subsequent public revelation of Guenevere's adultery and by Lancelot's refusal to grant mercy to a fellow knight (despicable as he is) in the judicial combat, even the best are shamed.

The last great exhibition of aristocratic pageantry is associated with the Queen's return to Arthur at the Pope's command. The Stanzaic *Morte*[6] (lines 2352–2371) provides an account of Lancelot and the Queen, dressed in white samite trimmed with silver, mounted on white steeds with ivory saddles and white saddle cloths made of Orient silk. They are accompanied by a hundred knights in green silk gowns, seated in jewelled saddles, and carrying olive branches in their hands. This is a charming evocation of a glamorous occasion but it cannot compare with Malory's carefully patterned expansion. Lancelot's hundred knights are dressed in green velvet and mounted on horses trapped in green velvet to their heels. Olive branches are carried 'in tokenyng of pees'. Guenevere is attended by twenty-four ladies dressed and mounted in the same style as the knights. Then there are twelve young gentlemen in white velvet with gold chains[7] mounted on twelve coursers elegantly trapped in velvet embroidered with pearls and other jewels to the number of a thousand. Lancelot and Guenevere are dressed alike in white cloth of gold tissue and extravagantly mounted. The display is not unlike that achieved by Louis XI, the Duke of Bourbon, on the state entry into Paris in 1461.[8] The hierarchic symbols of velvet, gold and precious stones are combined with the emotive symbols of white and green (purity and love). The pearl symbolises faith and innocence, the gold sovereignty and generosity, the olive branches are emblems of peace. The numbers, too, are significant.[9] A hundred and a thousand, multiples of ten, mean unity. Twelve and twenty-four combine the symbol of spiritual things, three, with that of material things, four. (Ironically, in cabalistic lore twelve represented sexual passion.) This procession, combining symmetry of form with images of light, is a public statement of the lovers' nobility, fidelity, honour and good intentions, but it ends in complete disaster.

Having ridden in splendid array from the Joyous Gard to Carlisle and entered the castle, Lancelot dismounts, helps the Queen down from her horse, and leads her to King Arthur before whom they both kneel as a sign of respect and submission. The King sits still and says no word. Lancelot makes an impassioned speech, reminding Arthur of all his past services:

> 'In justis and in turnements and in batayles set, bothe on horsebak and on foote, I have oftyn rescowed you, and you, my lorde sir Gawayne, and many mo of youre knyghtes in many dyvers placis'.
>
> (1198; Malory's addition)

This is all true enough. But to protect the Queen's honour, he also deliberately lies, knowing that he can support his claim by means of his superior prowess:

> 'And if there be ony knyght, of what degré that ever he be off, except your person, that woll sey or dare say but that she ys trew and clene to you, I here myselff, sir Launcelot du Lake, woll make hit good uppon hys body that she ys a trew lady unto you'.
>
> (1197)

Gawain, however, refuses to be pacified. The upshot of the return of Guenevere is that Lancelot is banished from court forever.

Malory's expansions of 'The Fair Maid of Astolat' and the return of Guenevere and his original creation of the maying scene are marked by an unusual specificity of imagery. The effect is a vivid pictorialism with philosophical and emotional overtones. As early as the twelfth century Hugh of St Victor linked the admiration of earthly beauty with regret for its mutability:

> Consider the well-laden caravan crossing the desert: thieves attack it, and nothing is left of it but blood and horror. Look at that beautiful palace: it is full of cares and anxiety. Consider this pretty girl: she is threatened by age, decrepitude, and death . . . And there lies the world, annihilated – that beautiful world whose grace we admired, whose beauty we praised, whose joy we desired.[10]

By the end of the Middle Ages, aestheticism expressed in what Huizinga calls 'the relish for pomp and display' was combined with 'a general feeling of impending calamity'.[11] Malory in his final books movingly evokes this atmosphere. Galahad's last message to his father – 'remembir of this worlde unstable' (original in Malory) – is a warning to the entire Arthurian society.

The change of mood from the joy and confidence of the first five books to the sadness and insecurity of the last may also be explained by the change of mode from romance to chronicle. Taking up again the biography of Arthur, Malory becomes more specific in his geography.[12] Astolat is identified with Guildford, the Joyous Gard with Alnwick or Bamborough, castles that the Warwickshire Malory would have seen during the Wars of the Roses.[13] The French lands which Lancelot distributes to his followers correspond closely to the political divisions of France in the second quarter of the fifteenth century.[14] Contemporary references abound, the most striking being the author's condemnation of English fickleness and his connection of Kent, Sussex, Surrey, Essex, and Norfolk with support for the usurper Mordred.[15]

Specific details of chronology give Book VIII the authority of an annal. Arthur's army waits outside the Joyous Gard for fifteen weeks before Lancelot can be persuaded to join battle. Lancelot is given fifteen days to leave England. At the siege of Benwick half a year passes before he comes out of his castle. Gawain takes three weeks to recover from his first wound and lies sick a month with his second. The exact details of Gawain's death day, even the hour of death, are revealed in letters to Arthur and Lancelot (Malory's addition). Nothing more clearly indicates the difference between romance and history than the repetition at the beginning of 'Slander and Strife' of May and winter imagery used in 'The Knight of the Cart' to define the nature of love:

> In May, whan every harte floryshyth and burgenyth (for, as the season ys lusty to beholde and comfortable, so man and woman rejoysyth and gladith of somer commynge with his freyshe floures, for wynter wyth hys rowghe wyndis and blastis causyth lusty men and women to cowre and to syt by fyres), so thys season hit befelle in the moneth of May a grete augur and unhappe that stynted nat tylle the floure of chyvalry of alle the worlde was destroyed and slayne.

(1161)

The ephemerality of May blossoms signifies the vulnerability of 'the floure of chyvalry of alle the worlde'. The outbreak of strife in May, a season of joy when used in a romantic context, takes no account of decorum.

There is increased realism in the treatment of castles which are no longer wish-fulfilling settings associated with courtly pleasures but centres of gossip and intrigue. Arthur shifts his court from Camelot, the ideal centre, to castles in London and Carlisle. To these real castles there come no boon seekers, no message bearing damsels and dwarfs, no defeated knights offered as tributes to Arthur and Guenevere. There is an obsession not with 'worship' but with shame. Lancelot tries to break away from court because, as he tells the Queen, 'the boldenesse of you and me woll brynge us to shame and sclaundir, and that were me lothe to se you dishonoured'. Agravain and Mordred use shame on the King's behalf to excuse their hatred of Lancelot and to stir up trouble in the King's chamber:

> 'I mervayle that we all be nat ashamed bothe to se and to know how sir Launcelot lyeth dayly and nyghtly by the quene. And all we know well that hit ys so, and hit ys shamefully suffird of us all that we shulde suffir so noble a kynge as kynge Arthur ys to be shamed'.

(1161)

'The Knight of the Cart' is a consistent record of dishonourable behaviour, with Meleagant's castle, only seven miles from Westminster, providing the chief setting. The kidnapping of the Queen and her unarmed retinue by a knight of the Round Table implies a disregard of courtesy that Guenevere indignantly points out:

> 'Traytoure knyght . . . what caste thou to do? Wolt thou shame thyseff? Bethynke the how thou arte a kyngis sonne and a knyght of the Table Rounde and thou thus to be aboute to dishonoure the noble kyng that made the knyght! Thou shamyst all knyghthode and thyselffe and me. And I lat the wyte thou shalt never shame me, for I had levir kut myne owne throte in twayne rather than thou sholde dishonoure me!'

(1122; original in Malory)

The intensity of Guenevere's condemnation is indicated by her use of the contemptuous second person singular pronoun.

Subsequent details contribute to the degradation of chivalric society – 'the attack on Lancelot's horse, the killing of the carter, the hero's ignominious arrival in a cart, the usual bickering between Lancelot and Guenevere, Meleagant's intrusion into the bedroom and throwing back of the curtains, the bloody sheets and pillow, the accusations of adultery and the shame felt by the wounded knights at the sight of the blood, the use of the trap-door to take Lancelot prisoner.

Lancelot's journey to rescue a beautiful lady from the castle of an evil knight is the only genuine quest undertaken by a Knight of the Round Table after the Grail Quest has ended. The quest begins in a conventional way with the lady in distress dispatching a ring-bearing messenger and the hero leaping onto his horse and riding off into the forest. But it soon becomes apparent that 'The Knight of the Cart' is a perversion of chivalric adventures in an ideal world.

Lancelot arrives at the castle not on horseback but in a cart, a means of transport with criminal associations since Guenevere's lady concludes that its occupant is going to be hanged. His horse follows, treading 'hys guttis and hys paunche undir hys feete'. Once inside the castle, the hero discovers that his lady has already made peace with her kidnapper. Lancelot's ironic reply is psychologically credible and totally unromantic:

> 'And, madame . . . and I had wyste that ye wolde have bene so lyghtly accorded with hym, I wolde nat a made such haste unto you'.
>
> (1129; Malory's addition)

The later coupling of the lovers also seems unromantic while the public revelation of Guenevere's adultery is certainly contrary to the secrecy required by the code of courtly love.

In 'Slander and Strife' the motif of entrapment, before associated only with evil castles, is attached to Arthur's castle at Carlisle where Mordred and his gang finally catch the lovers in Guenevere's bedroom after the king has sent word that he will stay in the forest to hunt. Lancelot escapes by killing all his assailants except Mordred but Guenevere, left behind, is judged to the stake. While rescuing her for the third time, Arthur's greatest knight unintentionally kills Gareth and Gaheris, drawing on himself Gawain's implacable vengeance. The association of treachery with the Carlisle castle is reasserted through Lancelot's fear that if he were to return Guenevere to the king as Tristram, after holding her for three years at the Joyous Gard, had returned Isolde to King Mark, he too might be murdered with a sharp spear in his back. Lancelot's own castles, Joyous Gard (renamed Dolorous Gard) and Benwick, become places of confinement where he and his followers are trapped not by Arthur's and Gawain's armies but by the hero's loyalty, courtesy, and affection for his king. For King Bagdemagus, Lancelot's courtesy is a source of shame. The allies denounce this hiding in holes, drooping within walls, and cowering in castles when there are battles to be fought. In Huizinga's words, the violent present has destroyed 'the perfection of an imaginary past.'[16]

The movement away from pure romance also affects the treatment of forests which in 'The Book of Sir Launcelot and Queen Guenevere' and 'The Morte Arthur' are closer to those of the Grail Quest than to the perilous forests of secular adventure. No longer is the deep forest an environment in which the knight's prowess is tested by encounters with giants, fées, and unknown challengers waiting at fords or wells. The only human habitations seem to be hermitages, places of asceticism, suffering, and self-examination. As in the 'Tale of the Sankgreal', the hermits are men of worship who from piety have accepted poverty, surrendering high office and extensive lands. Baldwin of Brittany has a hermitage in a wood near Winchester, beside a great cliff with a river running under it. Brastias dwells in Windsor forest near a burbling well.

The former Archbishop of Canterbury, having cursed the usurper Mordred in 'the moste orguluste wyse', becomes the priest-hermit of a chapel near Glastonbury.

The forest's religious ambience seems related to the theme of Lancelot's salvation. Of all the Grail knights who return to court, he alone has been marked by the experience: –

> hit may nat be yet lyghtly forgotyn, the hyghe servyse in whom I dud my dyligente laboure'.

> (1046; Malory's addition)

Even though the love affair continues 'hotter' than ever, his ability to heal Sir Urry proves that he still has God's grace. Banished from court by the jealous Guenevere, he withdraws not to his own Joyous Gard or some other hospitable castle but, on the advice of the successful Grail knight Bors, to Brastias' hermitage near Windsor. He returns only to fight in the judicial combat against Mador. Having been severely wounded by Bors in the tournament at Winchester, he is taken to Baldwin's hermitage where he is devotedly nursed by the hermit and Elaine. The terrible pain may be a form of expiation for the sins of the flesh; the wound itself an intervention of divine grace to keep him from the vices of adultery and homicide. From Our Lady Day in mid-August until All-hallowmass he is *hors de combat* and his return to court is further delayed by the reopening of his wound as he gallops about in the forest to exercise his horse.

Before the Great Tournament he again lodges with Brastias in Windsor Forest, spending his days not in knight-erranty but in resting beside a well. Here he is humiliatingly shot in the buttock by a huntress – 'and the wounde was passynge sore and unhappyly smytten, for hit was on such a place that he myght nat sytte in no sadyll'. The knight perceives that he seems fated to forego chivalric pursuits:

> 'A, mercy Jesu! . . . I may calle myselff the most unhappy man that lyvyth, for ever whan I wolde have faynst worshyp there befallyth me ever som unhappy thynge'.

> (1106; Malory's addition)

That the forest rather than the castle affords security, healing and eventual salvation is suggested by the conclusion of the *Morte Darthur*. Guenevere steals away from the Tower of London, which she had fortified against Mordred, to become a nun in the west country. Rejecting the realm in France which the queen refuses to share with him, Lancelot proceeds through a forest until he reaches the hermitage and chapel between two cliffs where he lives out a life of abstinence and sanctity. In medieval terms, the *Morte Darthur* has a happy ending. Arthur is splendidly buried at Glastonbury or taken to the vale of Avalon whence he will return to rule again. Political order is restored by the accession of Constantine. Guenevere wins salvation through fasting, prayers, and alms-deeds and Lancelot's salvation is confirmed by the archbishop's dream of angels carrying him to the open gates of heaven. The last knights of the Round Table die in the Holy Land fighting against the Turks.

With all these good ends, why are we left with a tragic sense of waste? For one thing, the dominant imagery of 'The Most Piteous Tale of the Morte Arthur Saunz Guerdon' is concerned with loss and desolation. Guenevere is stripped of her royal robes, involuntarily as she is led to the stake in her smock, voluntarily as she takes the nun's habit of black and white. In refusing to wear armour to escort Guenevere, Gareth and Gaheris in effect reject a chivalric life that no longer seems honourable. Lancelot is exiled from England and his French lands are burned and wasted by Arthur's invading army. Mordred despoils Arthur of his crown, his queen, his kingdom, and the greater part of his 'new-fangill' subjects. Pillagers and robbers on the battlefield at Salisbury strip the corpses, reducing the noble knights to mere unaccommodated man. Now truly are the best 'full colde at the harteroote'. No longer needed for quest and joust after their masters have put on monks' habits, the horses of Lancelot and his seven companions 'wente where they wolde, for they toke no regarde of no worldly rychesses'.

The terrible wounds which in the romantic world were easily healed, often by magic, now bear the expectancy of death. Gawain knows that his old wound will have him dead by noon. On the Day of Destiny, the rushing and riding, thrusting and striking that had once conveyed exuberant, life-promoting energy, now lay a hundred thousand noble knights to the cold earth. Mordred, feeling that he has his death wound, forces himself up to the burr of Arthur's spear and cleaves his father's skull. The most horrifying image of disintegration is Lucan with his foaming mouth, his guts falling out of his body and his bursting heart.

This pattern of physical loss and decay is appropriate to the theme of courtly disintegration, a theme that is eloquently voiced by the central characters. Arthur is sorrier for the loss of his good knights than of his queen: 'for quenys I myght have inow, but such a felyship of good knyghtes shall never be togydirs in no company'. The death of Gawain means an end of earthly joy, for with Lancelot and Gawain lay the king's happiness. Lancelot's hope of marrying Guenevere after her husband's death and taking her to his own kingdom is thwarted by her determination to end their relationship forever 'for thorow the and me ys the floure of kyngis and knyghtes destroyed'. To Bedevere's question, 'What shall become of me now that you are leaving me here alone among my enemies?' Arthur can only reply, 'Do as well as you can for there is no use trusting in me.' Relationships based on mutual affection and responsibility no longer unite the king and his wife, the king and his subjects, the knights of the Round Table or the courtly lovers. Virtually all the great speeches of lamentation and regret are original.[17]

In the *Morte Darthur* Malory depicts a world of castles and perilous forests, tournament grounds and battle fields almost exclusively populated by kings and queens, knights and ladies. It is a world where goodness is expressed not only by the distribution of lands, the provision of hospitality, the rescue of ladies, and the defeat of evil knights, giants, and fées but also by the offering of prayers, founding of monasteries, and taking of holy orders. The events of the first five books are controlled by the conventions of sovereignty, courtesy, secular knight-errantry and magic, conventions which operate in an idealised world removed from ordinary human experience. 'The Tale of the Sankgreal,' being an allegory of Christian lives, is equally idealised in its depiction of setting. In the two final books, however, the specificity of temporal and spatial details moves the characters (and the reader) forward in time from a distant and indeterminate golden age of chivalry to a finite period of English history. The fifteenth century had its glamour, too, as Malory's descriptions of Guenevere's maying and Lancelot's procession show, but the correspondence between these pageants and real courtly life[18] is a reminder that earthly beauty and joy are transient just as the references to treason, rebellion and usurpation are reminders that in fifteenth century England the feudal system has broken down. When Arthur, Lancelot and Guenevere are no longer wish-fulfilling models whose success is guaranteed by the conventions of romance but, instead, individuals caught in a dilemma that cannot be resolved by *la chevalerie terrienne*, then what a Spanish philosopher calls 'the tragic sense of life' permeates the milieu.

In spite of the main characters' apotheosis, it is the 'man of flesh and bone',[19] not the man of the philosophers and theologians who is closest to Malory's heart. The last statement of chivalric virtue is contained in Ector's eulogy of Lancelot delivered at the hero's castle, Joyous Gard. The author can find no better way of expressing excellence than by using the imagery of *la roiaume aventureux*. Juxtaposed to the anagogic images of the soul born towards the open gates of heaven by choirs of angels, the sweet fragrance given off by the body (the odour of sanctity), and the songs and bright lights in the choir, symbols of salvation, the eulogy brings us back to earth and, with its use of past tenses, reverses our perspective.

When William Caxton printed the *Morte Darthur* in 1485, he advertised the book by summarising its contents:

(It) treateth of the noble actes, feates of armes of chyvalrye, prowess, hardynesse, humanyté, love, curtosye, and veray gentylnesse, wyth many wonderful hystoryes and adventures (cxlvi).

Those who follow virtue, as Malory represents it, will enjoy fame and renown and, after this short and transitory life, everlasting bliss in heaven.

6

Patterns of Time

The diversity of late medieval temporal patterns is illustrated by Pieter Brueghel's painting 'The Triumph of Time' where a child-devouring Cronus, a serpent with its tail in its mouth, sun, moon, chariot, globe, clock, hourglass, zodiacal signs, church, maypole, leafy woods, bare boughs, the Tree of Life hung with the scales of the Last Judgment, Death with his scythe mounted on a horse that scatters the perishable artefacts of civilisation, and an angel sounding the last trump are combined to express linear, cyclical, and vertical concepts. Like the painting, Malory's *Morte Darthur* is typically medieval in its lack of a consistent historical perspective or a unified iconography. In the most literal sense, the time of Arthur's reign is the fifth century for his grandfather was the historical Constantine who proclaimed himself Roman Emperor at York in 306 AD. The genealogy is revealed and emphasised when Arthur rejects Lucius' claim to tribute. We are also given a fifth century date for the commencement of the Grail Quest: four hundred and fifty-four years after the Crucifixion. Malory says little about the Saxons – they are Mark's enemies rather than Arthur's – for the ethos of his historical vision is that of the high middle ages, evoked not only by political allusions to establishing the succession, the voice of the commons, the role of the Archbishop of Canterbury, trial by combat but also by reference to architecture, costume, arms and armour. Complexities and inconsistencies are partly due to the variety of his sources, partly to his own desire to update traditional material.

Castle architecture ranges from simple Norman towers to the Red Knight's fourteenth-century stronghold, machicolated and double-ditched. The monasteries of white monks so common in the Grail landscape would not have been found much before the thirteenth century. Allusions to clothing and armour are equally unreliable as indications that Arthurian society occupied a specific time. The long scarlet ermine-trimmed gowns of Lancelot, Tristram, and Galahad are typically thirteenth century and, in fact, often appear in illustrated French manuscripts of the period as both male and female garments. By the mid-fourteenth century a great change has occurred, the separation of male and female styles, with the man's surcoat becoming a short tunic, then a close-fitting jacket or doublet worn with hose. When Gawain tells Priamus that he has grown up in the wardrobe department of King Arthur's household where it is his duty to 'poynte all the paltokkys that longe to hymself and to dresse doublettis for deukys and erlys', the reference to doublets comes from Malory's fourteenth century source, the alliterative *Morte Arthure* (1. 2625), but he substitutes for the poet's 'aketoun' a fifteenth century term for the short tight tunic known as a paletot.

Isolde appears wimpled at the tournament at Lonezep, wearing the headgear of a respectable married woman of the thirteenth century, the period of Malory's source, the *Prose Tristan* (ca. 1232). Guenevere, too, seems to dress according to the old fashion of wearing two tunics, the *cotte* (kirtle), a long sometimes trailing garment with tight sleeves, and the sleeveless voluminous surcoat. When Lancelot finds the queen standing at the stake in her smock, he casts a kirtle and gown on her. The fact that the kirtle and gown can be put on so quickly suggests that they are loose thirteenth century garments rather than the more elaborate late fourteenth century styles that needed lacing, buttoning, and belting. Malory's depiction is more austere than that of the *Mort Artu* authors who send her out to die in a dress of red taffeta, a tunic, and a cloak. In the case of armour, the hauberk (chain mail shirt), the coif (a tight fitting mail cap), and the helm with ventails are thirteenth century while the helm with vizor, the gauntlet, and the horse armour (peytrels and crowpers) that bursts with the shock of Gareth's attack on the Red Knight are fourteenth century.

To the social milieu of his thirteenth and fourteenth century sources, Malory adds contemporary references. Professor Vinaver makes a case for Arthur's resemblance to Henry V and for similarities between the *Morte Darthur*'s military campaigns and those of the Hundred Years War and the Wars of the Roses in which Malory is thought to have participated.[2] There are business-like commercial details. Guenevere's search for the mad Lancelot costs her twenty thousand pounds; as mourning for Gawain, Lancelot doles out meat, fish, wine, ale and twelve pence to every comer. Mordred uses cannon, the latest military equipment, to attack the Tower of London.

Malorian patterns of time can best be explored by classifying them as linear, cyclical, and vertical. The Judeo-Christian linear scheme[3] envisaging time as a continuous progress from the Creation to the Last Judgment is applicable to the biography of an individual, the history of a nation, and the history of the Church. The history of Arthur is, in fact, inseparable from that of his nation and Church since he exemplifies the *Christianissimus rex*, an idealised type created by medieval historiographers[4] to justify the ambitions of Western successor states claiming the Roman *imperium* and to present a model of Christian kingship which embodied military successes against pagans, the protection and exaltation of the nation, and the upholding of justice.

Arthur's biography is not a day by day account or an annual report but an arbitrarily chosen sequence of events conforming to a hero pattern[5] – royal ancestry, mysterious conception and birth, protected childhood, success in a supernatural test followed by public recognition, preliminary combats, a crucial struggle, climactic victory, and apotheosis.

We see him as a new-born baby bound in a cloth of gold and delivered to Merlin at the postern gate, christened 'Arthur' by a holy man, and nursed by Sir Ector's wife 'with her owne pappe'. 'Yong' Arthur accompanies Ector and Kay to the New Year's Day tournament, succeeds in the sword test but is rejected by the barons as 'a boye of no hyghe blood borne' and as 'a berdles boye' (the noun having implications of social inferiority as well as youth). Youthful inexperience underlies his reliance on Merlin's strategic advice and, one feels, his seduction by Morgause (sent to spy on Arthur's court, as Malory tells us) but by the time of the Roman wars which occur about twenty years after the war with the Five Kings, he is in the prime of life. After the defeat of Lucius and the coronation in Rome, he becomes fixed in the cyclical time of courtly romance, performing strictly ceremonial roles, until Mordred's jealousy and Lancelot's disaffection propel him back into a linear time that recognises the inescapability of age and death. Even so, Malory avoids the *Mort Artu* specification of Arthur's age as ninety-two, dissociating connotations of physical and mental debility from his depiction of a vigorous, decisive monarch.

Other heroes – Lancelot, Galahad, Tristram – provide an impression of passing time for they are glimpsed as infants, as youths about to be knighted, and then as successful knights-errant whose eventual deaths are described directly or reported. Tristram is allowed an 'enfance' superficially realistic (though the seven year periods are archetypal) – a stepmother acquired when he is seven, education in France until he is fourteen, instruction in hunting, harping, hawking and terminology until he is eighteen, when he turns up at his uncle's court.

Individuals are linked to their family's past by genealogy. For example, the historicity of Lancelot's life is asserted by his vision of a man with a crown of gold (Joseph of Arimathea) accompanied by seven kings, Lancelot's ancestors Nappus, Nacien, Hellyas le Grose, Lysays, Jonas, Lancelot, and Ban. His son Galahad shares not only in this ancestry but in that of his mother who is descended from the Keepers of the Grail and King David.

Memory also connects past and present in a personal way. Gawain's recollections of his father's death motivate the vengeful murders of King Pellinore, Morgause, and Lamerok. Lancelot's grief at the Glastonbury tomb is made almost unbearable by his remembrance of Guenevere's beauty and nobility and of his own sinful pride that has laid low these two who were 'pereles that ever was lyvyng of Cristen people'. Though little used in the earlier books, the individual's ability to recall the past is a poignant device in the chronicle of the Round Table's disintegration and destruction, whether it is Arthur mourning over Gawain's corpse, Lancelot reminding the full court of how he and his friends have upheld the fellowship, or Gawain recalling Gareth's devotion to Lancelot who has slain him.

Another device creating a sense of temporal progress as well as curiosity and suspense is the use of prophecy, an important element in the Christian assimilation of the Old Testament. Merlin functions as an Old Testament prophet, warning, foretelling, and preparing for events that are to come. Some prophecies are specific and personal announcements of the future, a kind of fortune-telling. On the first night that Uther sleeps with Igraine he will beget a child. The child that Arthur has begotten on his sister will destroy him and all his knights. Balin will strike the Dolorous Stroke that will cause great vengeance. In the place where Lanceor and Columbe were slain, Lancelot and Tristram will fight the greatest battle between knights and true lovers ever seen. Balin's sword will never be handled by any except the best knight in the world, Lancelot or Galahad. Lancelot will kill Gawain. The most poignant prophecies concern his own fate which he can foresee but not avoid. Warnings to Arthur have the effect of prophecy; for example, the repeated warning about guarding his scabbard, and the disapproval of Arthur's plan to marry Guenevere, for 'Launcelot scholde love hir, and sche hym agayne'.

A second concentration of warnings and prophecies occurs in the story of the Grail. Hermits are the chief percipient agents, foreshadowing such things as the coming of Galahad and the instability of Lancelot, but diverse sources – Elaine, King Pelles, Josephé, the daughter of Duke Lyanowre, Perceval's sister, and even the tomb at Corbenic and the Ship of Solomon – contribute to the Providential nature of this tale.

The allegorical dream vision not only propels the action forward but creates an emotion of wonder, fear, or curiosity appropriate to the effect that the future event will have on the dreamer. Arthur's dream of the marvellous dragon destroying the diabolical bear presages his dual victory over the giant of St Michael's Mount and the forces of the Emperor Lucius. When the King of the Hundred Knights dreams that the castles and towns of the eleven rebel kings are blown down by a great wind and carried off in a flood, the confidence of Arthur's enemies is shaken and their destruction assured.

In the first two books, Malory's treatment of chronicle material is too often a sequence of actions crudely linked by temporal adverbs ('and then', 'and when'), the paratactic structure boringly emphasising the linearity. Nevertheless, such embellishments as prophecies, dream visions, magic tests and giant-slaying carry us along as Arthur establishes his kingdom and his empire which until the seventeenth century were regarded as historical realities.[6]

With the Grail material, the reign of Arthur and the lives of his knights are integrated into the larger scheme of Judeo-Christian world history. Galahad himself is a type of Christ, his adventures a re-enactment of Biblical history as he heals the blind king Mordrain, the Maimed King, and the cripple at Sarras or – in Harrowing of Hell parallels – leads the prisoners from the Castle of

Maidens and releases the souls from the burning tomb. The Grail is the vessel of the Last Supper, the lance the weapon with which the legendary Longinus pierced Christ's side. The history of these relics is part of an evangelisation myth that attributes to Joseph of Arimathea the founding of the British Church. White knights (angels), holy men, saintly recluses encountered by the Grail knights recreate church 'history' with their stories of King Evelake's war against the Saracens, Josephé's imprisonment in Great Britain and his release by Mondrames, the wounding of Nacien, the alternative version of the Dolorous Stroke and Waste Land.

The most powerful historical artifact, aside from the Grail is the Ship of Solomon, a complex synthesis of Biblical typology.[7] On its side is written 'I am Faythe'. In recounting its history and explaining its artefacts – the bed with its crown and richly mounted sword, the three spindles, one white for the purity of Eve undefiled and of the Virgin Mary, one green for procreation, one red for Abel's blood – Perceval's sister links contemporary history (the Grail Quest) to universal history. Furthermore, the history of an individual, Galahad, is joined to that of his ancestor Solomon who had been assured by a disembodied voice that 'the laste knyght of thy kynred shall reste in thys bedde'. This ship has its existence in time rather than space for it carries the history of man from his creation to the present.

Since the *Morte Darthur* begins in King Uther's time, a little before Arthur's conception, and ends when the last Round Table knights have died in the Holy Land, the linear time occupies about a hundred years. That the period had no exact historical identity would not have bothered Malory or most of his contemporaries who believed with Caxton that 'there was suche a noble kyng named Arthur, and reputed one of the nine worthy, and fyrst and chyef of the Cristen men'.

While a linear time scheme is appropriate to secular and religious history, cyclical time is appropriate to myth and romance for these are genres of renewal. Through the natural process of changeless change, every night, winter and death flows into day, spring and birth. The undiminished beauty of fées, the agelessness of knights and ladies, the terrible but never fatal wounds of heroes, the ability of villains like Tarquin, Carados and Breuze Sans Pyté to return from the dead and fight again testify to the renewal implicit in this pattern which predominates in 'The Noble Tale of Sir Launcelot du Lake,' 'The Tale of Sir Gareth of Orkney' and 'The Book of Sir Tristram de Lyones.' It is wrong to think of 'The Book of Sir Tristram' as later than the other two simply because it follows them. Lamerok, Dinadan, La Cote Male Tayle and Palomides are clearly established knights when they turn up at Lyoness' tournament. The begetting of Galahad in linear time may already have occurred when Lancelot begins the round of activities described in Book III.[8] Critics who attempt to construct a consistent chronology for the *Morte Darthur*[9] fail to recognise that the book accommodates more than one view of time.

Whether diurnal, seasonal, or epochal, withdrawal and return provide the rhythm of adventure. The diurnal cycle reveals antithetical worlds of knight-errantry. In the morning the hero rides into a forest where the daylight hours produce dangerous challenges; at nightfall he inevitably arrives at a castle, pavilion, manor or hermitage that refreshes him with food, entertainment, rest and possibly love. The seasonal cycle, too, dictates the rituals of his life. New knights are created in the spring; summer (from Whitsun to Michaelmas) is the season of quests; winter is spent in hunting and hawking, jousting and tourneying. Twelve months is the period allowed for completing a task. Knights like Iwain and Marhalt who complete their quests before the appointed time accept the hospitalilty of a lady or an earl, only returning to Camelot at Pentecost.

The liturgical cycle is introduced not so much for religious as for social reasons. In *Morte Darthur* the great feasts of the Church are primarily chivalric occasions with the joust of the Diamond occurring at Christmas, the knighting of King Pelles' nephew at Candlemas (February 2) and Alexander the Orphan on Our Lady Day in Lent (March 25); the Great Tournament is held on the Feast of the Purification of Our Lady and the Winchester tournament on Allhallow-mas Day (November 1). Since even circles require an ending and beginning (the snake with its tale in its mouth), Arthur's Pentecostal Feast is the point of stasis, combining fulfilment and expectation. At least thirteen separate feasts on this day are mentioned[10] including those associated with Arthur's corona-tion, his post-nuptial establishment of the Round Table and the first swearing of the Round Table oath, Lancelot's return to court after the adventures of Book III, the arrival at court of Pelleas and Nyneve, Marhalt, Gareth (who on the following Pentecost is knighted and undertakes the quest of Lady Lyo-ness), and La Cote Male Tayle (not to mention a whole procession of defeated knights), Galahad's filling of the Sege Perilous and the beginning of the Grail Quest, and finally the Healing of Sir Urry. Urged by Isolde, Tristram attends the significant Pentecostal feast preceding the Grail Quest and during this same festal season Palomides is christened. These two knights alone remain in cyclical time, the one by returning to Isolde at the Joyous Gard, the other by continuing his pursuit of the questing beast, rather than moving into the linear time of the Grail Quest. Through these annual celebrations when the knights renew their oaths and receive public acclaim for their achievements, both they and the reader are restored to a recognizable point in time. Pentecost precipi-tates by means of *geis*, boons, and challenges another cycle of quest and combat. And, finally, it combines the chivalric and Christian symbolism that characterized much Arthurian romance.

The self-contained 'Tale of Sir Gareth of Orkney' illustrates the uses of cyclical time in chivalric romance. The book begins as Arthur and his court celebrate Pentecost at Kynke Kenadowne 'uppon the sondys that marched nyghe Walys.' Arthur's *geasa* is satisfied by the appearance of a young stranger who is granted a year's meat and drink and the promise of two more gifts when Pentecost comes round again. The following year during the celebrations in Caerleon, having been awarded a quest and knighted by Lancelot, he sets out to free Lady Lyoness from the Red Knight of the Red Laundes and to prove his worthiness. The third Pentecost, also spent at Caerleon, is marked by the appearance of defeated knights who testify to Gareth's deeds of prowess accomplished during the preceding twelve months. Lady Lyoness' tournament on the following Lady Day (August 15) allows a public demonstration of Gareth's superiority while reuniting him with Arthur's court. The tale concludes with his marriage at Michaelmas (September 29), the end of the questing season. Thus a tale that seems diffuse and erratically episodic is actually controlled by a consistent temporal pattern.

The diurnal cycle is utilised with equal consistency. When Gareth leaves court on the second Pentecost, to follow the guide damsel Lynet, he kills three thieves and releases their prisoner who entertains him that night in his castle. Next morning Gareth rides into the forest, kills two opponents at a ford, approaches the black land at evensong, kills the Black Knight and dons his armour, then meets and defeats the Green Knight who provides him with his second night's lodging. The third morning, after mass and breakfast at the castle, Gareth again rides into the forest, approaches the Red Knight's castle, defeats his opponent after two hours and is again sheltered for the night. On the fourth morning he rides into the forest, approaches the city of Sir Persaunte of Inde, and engages the Blue Knight in the hope of defeating him within two hours after noon so that he can reach Lady Lyoness' castle, seven miles away, while it is still daylight. But the combat is prolonged until suppertime and Gareth spends the night in Persaunte's pavilion. On the fifth day he approaches the Castle Daungerous, spending the night in a hermitage. On the sixth day he fights the Red Knight of the Red Laundes, purposely initiating the conflict early in defiance of his opponent's solar strength which increases as the sun rises to its zenith. This time the jousting lasts an entire day until evensong and later. After the Red Knight's capitulation, ten days are spent resting in a pavilion so that the hero's wounds may heal. Then Lyoness orders Gareth to labour in worship for twelve months to prove his devotion (and to provide time for further adventures).

The regular alternation of day and night, adventure and rest, forest and castle is the continuum of this genre. In 'The Tale of Gareth' and even more in 'The Book of Sir Tristram' there is a temporal amplitude not found in the chronicle material.

That Malory saw Arthurian time as a golden age is evident in his idealisation of courtly life at Camelot and in his disparaging comments on the present as compared with the past. Amid the pessimism, social fluidity, feudal disintegration and political uncertainty of fifteenth century England, it would not be strange if he, like his printer Caxton, longed for the return of a time when knights did more than 'go to the Baynes and playe atte dyse'.[12] The essence of his chivalric vision is expressed in the oath of the Round Table knights, and in original comments such as that appended to 'The Great Tournament': 'And he that was curteyse, trew, and faythefull to hys frynde was that tyme cherysshed.'

His most famous original comment occurs in 'The Knight of the Cart' where the joyful renewal of nature in May is likened to the blossoming and burgeoning in human hearts:

> for than all erbys and treys renewyth a man and woman, and in lyke wyse lovers callyth to their mynde olde jantylnes and olde servyse, and many kynde dedes that was forgotyn by neclygence.   (1119)

But love nowadays is not as it used to be. In 'a lytyll blaste of wyntres rasure' we deface and destroy love, for in many people there is no stability. The contrasting imagery of May and winter is ironically reiterated to introduce the account of Agravain's plot against Lancelot which comes to a head a year after Guenevere's Maying.

Perhaps because a circle is aesthetically more satisfying than a line, the biography of Arthur, though essentially linear, reveals some cyclical patterning. The Roman Wars which occupy seven years of linear time are fitted into the liturgical cycle by the coincidence of major events with the sequence of Christian feasts and into the seasonal cycle by references to nature. The Roman legates interrupt the New Year's feast; Arthur's parliament is called after the utas of St Hilary (January 21); Lucius plans to arrive in France by Easter; Arthur rides to St Michael's Mount through a springtime landscape; the Emperor is killed in May; in Tuscany, Sir Florens and his fellowship tie their horses in a flowery meadow; Arthur reaches Lucerne at Lammas (August 1) descending into Lombardy when the vines are loaded with grapes (October); soon afterwards, the Roman senators are granted six weeks to prepare for the coronation which takes place at Christmas.

In the last book, Arthur's dream of falling from a throne on Fortune's Wheel into black water where he is seized by serpents, dragons and wild beasts presages the end of his life cycle as the return of Excalibur to the Otherworld signifies the end of his reign. Finally, Arthur's own journey to Avalon whence 'men say that he shall com agayne' places him in the cycle of eternal return.

Like the Middle English miracle plays, the *Morte Darthur* belongs to the time of grace,[13] the time in which man can prepare himself for eternity. Not only had God entered time to live as man in history, but through His death in time He had won for those men who lived between the Crucifixion and the Last Judgment the possibility of eternal life in bliss. Guenevere's determination to 'gete my soule hole' in the hope of seeing the blessed face of Christ and sitting

6. *At the command of the wounded King Arthur, Bedivere returns Excalibur to the water*. Mort Artu (*London, British Library, Add.MS 10294, f.94*)

on His right side at Domesday is perfectly consistent with the medieval relating of time to eternity.

One cannot understand either the Grail material or 'the dolorous death and departing out of this world of Sir Launcelot and Queen Guenevere' without accepting the concept of vertical interventions of the supernatural and timeless in the natural and temporal.[14] Corbenic, like a sacred mountain, is a vertical connection between earth and heaven, time and eternity, while the Grail which it houses but does not confine is a symbol of God's grace,[15] expressing His glory, sweetness, plenitude, healing powers, and accessibility to the devout. Otherworld interventions persist throughout 'The Tale of the Sankgreal' as angels and devils encourage or tempt the questers, strange voices instruct and warn, and a hand without a body suddenly appears, holding a candle and bridle or seizing the Grail and lance for which the world has grown too evil. The healing of Sir Urry, Lancelot's triple vision charging him for the remission of his sins to attend to Guenevere's burial, and the archbishop's view of angels carrying Lancelot's soul to the open gates of heaven are other examples of the divine participating in the human.

Magic may also be seen as vertical intervention. When Lancelot is tricked into sleeping with Elaine to engender Galahad, Malory makes it clear that he is not simply confused by Brusen's drink, as in the French source, but that the enchantress has cast a spell that can only be broken by the light of day. Inasmuch as Galahad's conception is essential to the typological pattern, Brusen is a divine agent. Similarly, Merlin's use of magic to bring about Arthur's conception and the devising of the sword test to establish his claim to the throne are interventions seemingly ordained by God since Merlin counsels the Archbishop to summon the lords of the realm

> that they shold to London come by Christmas upon payne of cursynge, and for this cause, that Jesu that was borne on that nyghte, that He wold of His grete mercy shew some myracle, as He was come to be Kynge of mankynde, for to shewe somme myracle who shold be rightwys kynge of this reame. (12)

It is ironical and for the modern reader moving that despite Malory's acceptance of a conclusion asserting that asceticism, prayer, and withdrawal are preferable to the transient joys of earthly chivalry, nevertheless the author's expression of value remains mundane. The images in Ector's eulogy are entirely temporal and ephemeral – the knight bestriding his horse, bearing his shield, striking with his sword, setting his spear in its rest, sitting in the hall among ladies, making love to his woman, forgiving his opponents, cherishing his friends. All are victims of time. And yet they are what signify the noble and joyous.

The disjunction between the idealistic earlier books, with their confident

113

accounts of secular chivalric adventures, and the realistic final books is caused by a shift in the temporal frame. When Arthur's kingdom becomes a metaphor for fifteenth-century England with its continental wars, dynastic conflicts and disintegrating feudalism, there is a generic change from romance (which Northrop Frye has described as the 'mythos of Summer') to tragedy, the myth of a paradise lost.[16] The 'joy of the court,' an adumbration of the ideal world, is destroyed by envy, hatred, and treachery. In this situation, the only acceptable happy ending for characters living in linear (i.e. historical) time is provided by the allegorical image of human life as a pilgrimage or quest directed towards a heavenly state which Boethius described as 'interminabilis vitae tota simul et perfecto possessio.'[17] This is the solution offered by the authors of the *Vulgate Prose Cycle*. Whether or not Malory preferred *la chevalerie terrienne* to *la chevalerie célestienne*, his *Tale of the Sankgreal* is the *Morte Darthur's* pivot, accounting not only for the destruction of Arthur's earthly *roiaume aventureux* but also for the apotheosis which was the goal of every good Christian. As the Apocalypse promised, 'The kingdoms of this world are become the kingdoms of our Lord, and of his Christ.'

Notes

1: *The Sword and the Crown*

1. Bibliographical material on the origins of Arthur may be found in J. D. Bruce, *The Evolution of Arthurian Romance*, 2nd ed. (Gloucester, Mass., 1958), II, pp. 381–98; *Arthurian Literature in the Middle Ages*, ed. R. S. Loomis (London, 1959), *passim*; E. K. Chambers, *Arthur of Britain*, 2nd ed. (Cambridge, 1964), pp. 283–94. Other works on the historical Arthur include Geoffrey Ashe, ed. *The Quest for Arthur's Britain* (London, 1968); Beram Saklatvala, *Arthur: Roman Britain's Last Champion*; (Newton Abbot, 1967), and Richard Barber, *The Figure of Arthur* (London, 1972).

2. *Historia Regum Britanniae*, ed. Acton Griscom, trans. R. E. Jones (London, 1929); *Variant Version*, ed. Jacob Hammer (Cambridge, Mass., 1951); *The History of the Kings of Britain*, trans. Lewis Thorpe (Harmondsworth, 1966); hereafter referred to as *HRB*.

3. On Charlemagne as a source for Arthur see J. D. Bruce, I, p. 24; E. K. Chambers, 38, 72, 86 *et al.*; R. H. Fletcher, *The Arthurian Material in the Chronicles* (New York, 1966); p. 84; J. S. P. Tatlock, *The Legendary History of Britain* (Berkeley and Los Angeles, 1950), pp. 310–11; G. H. Gerould, 'King Arthur and Politics,' *Speculum II* (1927), 38ff.

4. Fletcher, pp. 109–12; Tatlock, pp. 308–9.

5. See William Matthews, *The Tragedy of Arthur* (Berkeley and Los Angeles, 1960), pp. 184–92.

6. Vinaver's Introduction to *The Works of Sir Thomas Malory* (Oxford, 1967), I, xxxi–xxxii.

7. Cf. *Pageant of the Birth, Life, and Death of Richard Beauchamp, Earl of Warwick*, ed. Viscount Dillon and W. H. St John Hope (London, 1914).

8. See Nellie Slayton Aurner, 'Sir Thomas Malory – Historian?' *PMLA*, xlviii (1933), 360–91.

9. *The Medieval World: Europe 1100–1350*, trans. Janet Sondheimer (London, 1962), p. 134.

10. Cf. Fitzroy Richard Somerset, Lord Raglan, *The Hero, A Study in Tradition, Myth and Drama* (London, 1936), pp. 178–80, 188. Re Arthur's resemblance to Alexander, see Matthews, *op. cit.*, pp. 32–67 and George Carey, *The Medieval Alexander* (Cambridge, 1956).

11. On Trojan genealogy, see T. D. Kendrick, *British Antiquity* (London, 1970 [1950]), p. 3; George Gordon, 'The Trojans in Britain,' *Essays of the English Association*, IX (1924), 9–30; Margaret R. Scherer, *The Legends of Troy in Art and Literature* (New York, 1963).

12. On Avalon as a Celtic Otherworld, see R. S. Loomis, 'The Legends of Arthur's Survival,' *ALMA*, pp. 64–7; H. R. Patch, *The Otherworld According to Descriptions in Medieval Literature* (New York, 1970 [1950]), pp. 284–7: L. A. Paton, *Studies in the Fairy Mythology of Arthurian Romance* (Boston, 1903; rptd. New York, 1959), pp. 25–48.

13. The 'Briton hope,' according to Tatlock (pp. 204–5) is the only evidence of popular familiarity with Arthur before *HRB*.

14. E. K. Chambers, *op. cit.*, p. 81.

15. J. Bédier, *Revue des deux mondes* LVII (1891), p. 860, cited by P. Rickard, *Britain in Medieval French Literature* (Cambridge, 1956), p. 76, fn. 1.

16. Elspeth M. Kennedy, 'King Arthur in the First Part of the Prose Lancelot,' *A Medieval Miscellany presented to Eugene Vinaver*, ed. F. Whitehead, A. H. Diverres, F. E. Sutcliffe (Manchester and New York, 1965), pp. 186–95.

17. John Leland, *Assertio Arturii*, cited by Fletcher, pp. 8–9.

18. Among the doubters of Geoffrey's reliability were William of Newburgh, Giraldus Cambrensis, Ralph Higden and his translator Trevisa, and Polydore Virgil.
19. In 1190, at a time when Henry II's Celtic subjects were cherishing the hope of Arthur's return, the grave of Arthur and Guenevere was conveniently found at Glastonbury soon after the discovery of a leaden cross bearing the inscription, 'Hic jacet Sepultus Inclytus Rex Arturus in Insula Avallonia;' cf. Giraldus Cambrensis, *De Principis Instructione* viii, 126–9 (ca. 1194). See also C. A. Ralegh Radford's 'Glastonbury Abbey,' *The Quest for Arthur's Britain*, pp. 119–38 which indicates that enthusiastic supporters of Arthur's historicity still exist.
20. The discovery of Gawain's tomb is mentioned by William of Malmesbury, by the *Flores Historiarum* compiled at St Albans ca. 1200 and by the Chronicle of the Monastery of Hales (ca. 1314). Cf. Malory's allusion to the burial of Gawain at Dover, *Works*, p. 1232.
21. 'Arthur's Round Table,' first described by the chronicler Hardyng ca. 1450, may still be seen at Winchester; cf. R. S. and L. H. Loomis, *Arthurian Legends in Medieval Art* (New York and London, 1938), p. 40. Recent scientific tests conducted by a team of experts under the direction of Martin Biddle have shed new light on the table's age and history.
22. For the association of Arthurian characters and artefacts with particular geographic settings see Giraldus Cambrensis, *Itinerarium Kambriae*; John Leland, *Assertio Arturii*, Michael Drayton, *Poly-Olbion*. Caxton's preface is reproduced in Vinaver's edition, pp. cxliii–cxlvii.
23. R. H. Hanning, *The Vision of History in Early Britain* (New York and London, 1966), p. 40.
24. See R. S. Loomis, *Arthurian Legends in Medieval Art* (London and New York, 1938), pp. 38–40 and figs. 11–17.
25. *The Survival of Geis in Medieval Romance* (Halle, 1933), p. 67. Reinhard cites as analogies such Irish legends as *Serglige Cuculainn*, *Cath Maige Tured*, and *Baile in Scáil* where swords and stones act as sentient beings with power to determine man's fate.
26. An interesting analogy is provided by a window in the North Choir Aisle of York Minster where King Athelstan is shown laying his sword on St John's altar. The glass is dated ca. 1423–32.
27. *Works*, p. 1287 fn. 16, 10, 11, 22; 20–3; 25–30.
28. E. R. Curtius, *European Literature and the Latin Middle Ages*, trans. W. R. Trask (New York and Evanston, 1953), p. 172.
29. Hanning, *op. cit.*, p. 155
30. *Morte Arthure*, ed. E. Brock, EETS–OS, No. 8 (London, 1871).
31. On the parallel historical situation under the Angevins see G. O. Sayles, *The Medieval Foundations of England* (London, 1966), pp. 325–9.
32. Cf. Mary E. Dichmann, 'The Tale of King Arthur and the Emperor Lucius,' *Malory's Originality*, ed. R. M. Lumiansky (Baltimore, 1964), pp. 74–9.
33. *HRB* X, ii; *Allit. M.A.* 11. 644–92.
34. *Works*, pp. 1367–8.
35. George B. Parks, 'King Arthur and the Roads to Rome,' *JEGP* XLV (1946), 164–70.
36. On the belief that dreams foretell future events and on the role of allegory in prophetic dreams see Constance B. Hieatt, *The Realism of Dream Visions* (The Hague–Paris, 1967). Arthur's dream, an enduring part of the chronicle tradition, occurs in *HRB*, X, ii, Wace, XX, 528ff. Layamon 25, 500ff, Robert of Gloucester 4146ff. Malory's version follows his source closely – Allit. M.A. 758–831.
37. See J. S. P. Tatlock, 'The Dragons of Wessex and Wales,' *Speculum*, viii (1933), 223–35.
38 *HRB* vii, 3 and viii, 15.
39. Paris, B.N. MS Fr. 95, fol. 173ᵛ and 327ᵛ. On *armes parlantes* involving a pun on an individual's name, see Gerard J. Brault, *Early Blazon, Heraldic Terminology in the Twelfth and Thirteenth Centuries with Special Reference to Arthurian Literature* (Oxford, 1972), p. 23.
40. Cited by Tatlock, 'The Dragons of Wessex and Wales,' p. 226.
41. Enamelling, the process by which coloured glass was fused onto a metallic base, was a favourite technique of the medieval jeweller.
42. On medieval aesthetic theory, see Edgar de Bruyne, *Etudes d'esthétique médiévale* (Brugge, 1946), 3 vols. and Eileen B. Hennessy's one volume abridgement and translation, *The Esthetics of the Middle Ages* (New York, 1969).
43. Fletcher, p. 90. Tatlock's contrary view, pp. 87–8, is not really convincing in view of the fact that giant-killing or monster-killing was a motif in many mythological traditions.

44. *HRB* x, iii.
45. Northrop Frye, *Anatomy of Criticism* (New York, 1966), p. 147.
46. Rosemond Tuve, *Allegorical Imagery: Some Medieval Books and Their Posterity* (Princeton, 1966), p. 189.
47. See John Finlayson, ed. *Morte Arthure* (London, 1967), pp. 16–18 and 'Arthur and the Giant of St. Michael's Mount,' *Medium Aevum*, xxxii (1963), 112–20.
48. In *HRB*, X, iii, the church is built as a memorial to Hoel's niece.
49. Cf. Tatlock, pp. 113ff; Carey, *The Medieval Alexander, passim*. According to Saklatvala, *op. cit.*, p. 49, the list of Arthur's enemies is analogous to the allies of Theodosius who helped the Emperor of the East defeat Maximus at Aquileia in 388 AD. Saklatvala regards Maximus, who was proclaimed Emperor by the army in Britain in 383 AD and then invaded the continent, as a prototype of Arthur.
50. According to Hanning, p. 49, the national historians of Western Europe, e.g., Jordanes and Gregory of Tours, sought to dignify their own nations by showing them to be worthy inheritors of the Roman Empire and culture. Geoffrey's Arthur may be the product of a similar motivation. See also Stephen Medcalf ed. 'On reading books from a half-alien culture,' *The Later Middle Ages* (London, 1981), pp. 89–90.
51. Caxton's text, Bk. V, Ch. 1. This detail does not occur in the Alliterative *Morte Arthure* but is found in Geoffrey's *HRB* IX, xv.
52. Cf. Alliterative *Morte Arthure* 11. 2026–7.
53. Cf. *Alliterative Morte Arthure* 11. 2948–88; 3034–43.
54. See Vinaver's note on 245, 4–8, p. 1405.
55. See Erich Auerbach's 'The Knight Sets Forth' in *Mimesis, the Representation of Reality in Western Literature*, trans. Willard R. Trask (Princeton, 1953), pp. 132–3.
56. See Ernest C. York, 'Legal Punishment in Malory's *Morte Darthur*', *English Language Notes* 11 (1973), 14–21.
57. On analogies between the judicial combats in Malory's source, *La Mort le roi Artu*, and in feudal France up to the mid-thirteenth century, see R. Howard Bloch, 'From Grail Quest to Inquest: The Death of king Arthur and the Birth of France,' *MLR* 69 (1974), 40–55. See also Ernest C. York, 'The Duel of Chivalry in Malory's Book xix', *Philological Quarterly*, XLVIII (1969), 186–91. Trial by battle remained part of the law of England until the nineteenth century. See W. S. Holdsworth, *A History of English Law* (London, 1931), 5 vols., vol. 1, pp. 308–10.
58. *Works*, pp. 1632–3, n. 1174. 18; 28–9. Cf. also Elizabeth T. Pochoda, *Arthurian Propaganda, Le Morte Darthur as an Historical Ideal of Life* (Chapel Hill, 1971), p. 81: 'The emphasis on justice as the first and most important obligation of the king is another echo of contemporary political thought. Fortescue, recalling the coronation oath, described justice as the primary obligation of the crown and the sole means of its perpetuation.'
59. See R. H. Fletcher, *op. cit.*, on the treatment of the theme by Geoffrey of Monmouth, Wace, Layamon, Robert Mannyng, Jehan de Wavrin *et al.*
60. The most important source for medieval views of Fortune was Boethius' *De Consolatione Philosophiae*. For critical studies, see H. R. Patch, *The Goddess Fortuna in Medieval Literature* (Cambridge, Mass., 1927), F. P. Pickering, *Literature and Art in the Middle Ages* (Florida, 1970), pp. 168–222; and Philippa Tristram, *Figures of Life and Death in Medieval English Literature* (London, 1976), pp. 128–47.
61. Two interesting thirteenth century examples of the motif are Villard de Honnecourt's six figure schema reproduced in the facsimile edition, *Album de Villard de Honnecourt, architecte du XIII* siècle, ed. Léonce Laget (Paris, 1968), plate XLI; and the mural on the north choir wall of Rochester Cathedral.
62. On the discovery of Arthur's tomb at Glastonbury, see C. A. Ralegh Radford, 'Glastonbury Abbey' in *The Quest for Arthur's Britain*, ed. Geoffrey Ashe (London, 1968), pp. 119–38; Richard Barber, *The Figure of Arthur* (London, 1972), pp. 126–34; E. K. Chambers, *Arthur of Britain; the Story of King Arthur in History and Legend* (London, 1966 [1927]), pp. 112–27; and J. A. Robinson, *Two Glastonbury Legends* (Cambridge, 1926), pp. 8–17. The same critics discuss the identification of Glastonbury with Avalon as does Geoffrey Ashe in *King Arthur's Avalon* (London, 1957).
63. Cf. R. S. Loomis, 'The Legend of Arthur's Survival,' *ALMA*, pp. 64–71; E. K. Chambers,

op. cit., pp. 121–3, 219–32; R. H. Fletcher, *op. cit.*, pp. 100–2; H. R. Patch, *The Otherworld*, pp. 284–7; L. A. Paton, *op. cit.*, pp. 25–48.

64. Cf. the Irish *imrama* such as *The Voyage of Bran* and *The Lad of the Ferule*; the OF lay of *Guingamor*, the OF romance of Ogier the Dane and the English ballad of Thomas the Rymer.
65. The words were found on Arthur's tomb at Glastonbury when it was opened in 1278 at the order of Edward I. The words also appear in the Thornton MS at the end of the Alliterative *Morte Arthure*, added, says Benson in *King Arthur's Death, The Middle English Stanzaic Morte Arthur and Alliterative Morte Arthure* (Indianapolis and New York, 1974), p. 238, not by the original author but by a later reader.

2: Castles, Courts and Courtesy

1. Rose Macaulay, *The Pleasure of Ruins*, ed. Constance B. Smith (London, 1964), p. 266.
2. Erich Auerbach, *Mimesis, the Representation of Reality in Western Literature*, trans. Willard R. Trask (Princeton, 1953), p. 131.
3. On fairy mistresses and journeys to fairyland, see A. C. L. Brown, *The Origin of the Grail Legend* (New York, 1943), ch. I and II; H. R. Patch, *The Other World According to Descriptions in Medieval Literature* (Cambridge, Mass., 1950), Ch. II and VII; Lucy A. Paton, *Studies in the Fairy Mythology of Arthurian Romance*, 2nd ed. (New York, 1960).
4. The displacement of Celtic myth is also effected by Malory's specific localisations. Camelot is identified with Winchester, the Joyous Gard with Alnwick or Bamborough, Astalot with Guildford and the castle of Magouns with Arundel.
5. See R. S. Loomis, *Celtic Myth and Arthurian Romance* (New York, 1927), ch. XVII; Jean Marx, *La Légende Arthurienne et Le Graal* (Paris, 1952).
6. Cf. Vinaver's note 824.16, *Works*, p. 1530: 'It is only in M's account that Brusen appears as an enchantress. Lancelot speaks of her (p. 796) as being the cause of the 'enchantment between him and Elaine', whereas in F she does no more than serve the magic drink which causes Lancelot to mistake Elaine for Guinevere.'
7. This is a good example of the rationalisation of Otherworld castles. In Chrétien de Troyes' *Le Chevalier de la Charrette*, such motifs as the sword and the water bridge and the *terre gaste* are probably survivals of a Celtic story about an abduction to the Otherworld. See T. P. Cross and W. A. Nitze, *Lancelot and Guenevere* (Chicago, 1930). In the Vulgate *Lancelot*, the hero must cross the sword bridge and confront lions that have been produced by magic. Malory's treatment is realistic, for Meleagant's castle exhibits no Otherworld features.
8. J. Huizinga, *The Waning of the Middle Ages, a Study of the Forms of Life, Thought, and Art in France and the Netherlands in the XIVth and XVth Centuries* (New York, 1954), p. 84. Other works dealing with the relationship between the historical and the literary tournament are Larry D. Benson, *Malory's Morte Darthur* (Cambridge, Mass., 1976), pp. 163–85; *La forme quon tenoit des tournoys et assemblees au temps du roy Uterpendragon et du roy Artus*, ed. Edouard Sandoz, 'Tourneys in the Arthurian Tradition,' *Speculum*, 19 (1944), 389–420; Robert C. Clephan, *The Tournament, Its Periods and Phases* (New York, 1967 [1919]); Ruth H. Cline, 'The Influence of Romances on Tournaments of the Middle Ages,' *Speculum*, 20 (1945), 204–11; Arthur B. Ferguson, *The Indian Summer of English Chivalry, Studies in the Decline and Transformation of Chivalric Idealism* (Durham, North Carolina, 1960), pp. 13–17, 22–24; R. S. Loomis, 'Arthurian Influence on Sport and Spectacle,' *Arthurian Literature in the Middle Ages*, ed. R. S. Loomis (Oxford, 1959), pp. 553–9.
9. Robert R. Hellenga, 'The Tournaments in Malory's Morte Darthur,' *Forum for Modern Language Studies*, X (1974), 67–78.
10. Noel Denholm-Young, 'The Tournament in the Thirteenth Century,' *Studies in Medieval History Presented to Frederick Maurice Powicke*, ed. R. W. Hunt, W. A. Pantin, R. W. Southern (Oxford, 1948), p. 240.
11. In fact, the violence of Malory's description surpasses that in his source, the Vulgate *Lancelot*. See H. Oskar Sommer, ed., *The Vulgate Version of the Arthurian Romances*, vol. V, 'Le Livre de Lancelot del Lac,' p. 101.
12. Miniatures of ladies watching from castles as knights joust are common in illustrated manuscripts. Cf. Paris, B.N., MS fr. 1453, fol. 39. In the fourteenth century, ivory caskets and mirror cases often depicted this motif, with the castle sometimes being designated as a

Castle of Love through the use of roses as ammunition. Examples are to be found in the Victoria and Albert Museum, London, and in the Louvre, Paris.

13. F. Flutre, *Tables des noms propres* (Poitiers, 1962), cites a number of thirteenth-century French romances in which Camelot is the residence of Arthur; e.g. *Artur, Claris, Floriant, L'Estoire del Graal, prose Lancelot, Meliador, Meliadus, Estoire del Merlin, Mort Artu, Perceval, Perlesvaus, Prophecies of Merlin, prose Tristran, Le Roman de Balain, Histoire de Giglan, La Queste de Saint Graal.*

14. *Il Dittamondo e le rime*, ed. G. Corsi (Barri, 1952), 1, iv, 22, cited in *Arthurian Literature in the Middle Ages*, ed. R. S. Loomis (Oxford, 1959), p. 422.

15. Ed. W. A. Nitze and T. A. Jenkins (Chicago, 1932), I, p. 25; 11. 67–77.

16. Henri Dupin, *La Courtoisie au Moyen Age (d'après les textes du XIIᵉ et du XIIIᵉ siècle)*, (Paris, 1906). On the historical importance of courtesy, see Diane Bornstein, *Mirrors of Courtesy* (Hamden, Conn. 1975) and Otto Cartellieri, *The Court of Burgundy, Studies in the History of Civilization* (London and New York, 1929). On courtesy in Middle English Literature see *Patterns of Love and Courtesy, Essays in Memory of C. S. Lewis*, ed. John Lawlor, especially D. S. Brewer's 'Courtesy and the Gawain-Poet,' pp. 54–85 and R. T. Davies' 'The Worshipful Way in Malory,' pp. 157–77.

17. In *Amour Courtois et Table Ronde* (Geneva, 1973), Jean Frappier maintains that 'la courtoisie du Moyen Age est beaucoup plus qu'un code de politesse et de galanterie. Elle englobe aussi un art d'aimer' (p. 2). A contrary view is taken by Alexander J. Denomy in 'Courtly Love and Courtliness,' *Speculum*, XXVIII (1953), 44–63, an essay which makes a distinction between *cortezia*, 'an ideal and a virtue of the courtly lover,' and *courtoisie*, 'the virtue and the ideal of the chevalier.' Of the Gawain-poet's view of courtesy, D. S. Brewer writes that the concept includes beauty, politeness, humour, self-control, bravery, and cleanliness but not *fine amour*. Malory's view of love has been discussed by Charles Moorman, 'Courtly Love in Malory,' *ELH*, XXVII (1960), 163–70 and P. E. Tucker, 'Chivalry in the Morte,' *Essays on Malory*, ed. J. A. W. Bennett (Oxford, 1963), 64–103. See also D. Van de Voort, *Love and Marriage in the English Medieval Romance* (Nashville, 1938).

18. Malory omits the elaborately detailed description of the feast in his source, the alliterative *Morte Arthure*, 11. 176–219.

19. On the question of Malory's responsibility for the content of the tale, see Vinaver, *Works*, pp. 1427–34; Wilfred L. Guerin, '"The Tale of Gareth": the Chivalric Flowering' in *Malory's Originality*, ed. R. M. Lumiansky (Baltimore, 1963), pp. 99–117; Larry D. Benson, *Malory's Morte Darthur* (Cambridge, Mass., 1976), pp. 92–108; Violet D. Scudder, *Le Morte Darthur of Sir Thomas Malory* (London, 1921), pp. 217–18; R. H. Wilson, 'The Fair Unknown in Malory,' *PMLA*, 58 (1943), 2–21; R. S. Loomis, 'Malory's Beaumains,' *PMLA*, 54 (1939), 656–68. P. J. C. Field, 'The Source of Malory's Tale of Gareth,' in *Aspects of Malory*, ed. Toshiyuke Takamiya & Derek Brewer (Cambridge, 1981), pp. 57–70.

20. This explanation is given in the Vulgate *Merlin*, Sommer, vol. II, p. 320.

21. Dupin, *op. cit.*, p. 15.

22. This is D. S. Brewer's word. See 'The Present Study of Malory,' *Arthurian Romance*, ed. D. D. R. Owen (Edinburgh and London, 1970), p. 88 and Brewer's introduction to *Malory: The Morte Darthur*, parts seven and eight (Evanston, 1970), pp. 12–19.

23. *Malory: The Morte Darthur*, pp. 15–18.

24. P. J. C. Field, *Romance and Chronicle, a Study of Malory's Prose Style* (London, 1971), p. 104.

3: The Perilous Forest

1. In Alison Stones' list of historiated initials in MS Rennes 255, 'The Earliest Illustrated Prose Lancelot Manuscript,' *Reading Medieval Studies*, III (1977), Appendix B, 36–41, out of 27 historiated initials illustrating *Lancelot*, 13 show a knight-errant on horseback.

2. On Malory's view of chivalry, see P. E. Tucker, 'Chivalry in the *Morte*,' *Essays on Malory*, ed. J. A. W. Bennett (Oxford, 1963), pp. 64–103.1 This chapter deals only with the adventures of *la chevalerie terrienne*. *La chevalerie celestienne* is the subject of chapter 4.

3. Gervase Mathew, 'Ideals of Knighthood in Late-Fourteenth-Century England,' *Studies in Medieval History Presented to Frederick Maurice Powicke*, ed. R. W. Hunt, W. A. Pantin, R. W. Southern (Oxford, 1948), p. 362.

4. J. R. R. Tolkien, 'On Fairy-Stories,' in *Tree and Leaf* (London, 1964), pp. 44–5.
5. Oliver Rackham, *Trees and Woodland in the British Landscape* (London, 1976), pp. 66–93. The original wildwood had all disappeared by 1250 (p. 64).
6. W. G. Hoskins, *The Making of the English Landscape* (London, 1960), p. 69. Hoskins speaks of a thick oak and ash forest covering much of England, with beech woods on the chalk and limestone uplands and elm, maple and silver birch in the lowlands.
7. Geoffrey of Monmouth, *Vita Merlini*, ed. Basil Clarke (Cardiff, 1973), vs. 908–942.
   The apple is an otherworld fruit associated with the love of a fée in many Irish tales; for example, the *Voyage of Bran*, the *Voyage of the Hui Corra*, the *Adventure of Cian's Son Teigue*, *Cormac's Adventures in the Land of Promise* and the *Adventures of Connla the Fair*. H. R. Patch, *The Other World According to Descriptions in Medieval Literature* (Cambridge, Mass., 1950), pp. 27–59.
8. Eugene Vinaver, *The Rise of Romance* (London, 1971), p. 69.
9. On the appearance of an Old Man as a warning of imminent death, see Philippa Tristram, *Figures of Life and Death in Medieval English Literature* (London, 1976), p. 70.
10. The fatal effect of 'death naming' is a widespread folkloric motif. See Sir James G. Frazer, *The Golden Bough, A Study in Magic and Religion* (New York, 1944), pp. 244–8; J. A. MacCulloch, ed., *The Mythology of All Races*, vol. 12 (New York, 1964), p. 201.
11. See Alwyn and Brinley Rees, *Celtic Heritage, Ancient Tradition in Ireland and Wales* (London, 1961), pp. 326–41 on the Irish hero's foreknowledge, through omens, of impending doom.
12. See A. O. H. Jarman, 'The Welsh Myrddin Poems,' in *Arthurian Literature in the Middle Ages*, ed. R. S. Loomis (Oxford, 1959), pp. 20–30.
13. *La Suite du Merlin*, a thirteenth century French prose romance is preserved in London, British Museum Ms. Add. 38117 and Cambridge University Library Ms. Add. 7071. There is also a fairly literal translation, the English *Prose Merlin* dating from about 1450 (Cambridge Universtiy Library MS FfIII 11); edited H. B. Wheatley, EETS x, xxi, xxxvi, cxii (1865, 1866, 1869, 1899).
14. Myles Dillon and Nora Chadwick, *The Celtic Realms* (London, 1967). See also Lucy A. Paton, *Studies in the Fairy Mythology of Arthurian Romance*, (New York, 1970 [1903]), pp. 4–5.
15. On the derivation of the name see R. S. Loomis, *Wales and the Arthurian Legend* (Cardiff, 1956), pp. 99ff; Lucy A. Paton, pp. 9–12; John Rhys, *Celtic Folklore* (Oxford, 1901), p. 373.
16. 'Thomas Rymer' in *English and Scottish Popular Ballads*, ed. Helen Child Sargent and George Lyman Kittredge (Boston, 1904), pp. 63–6.
17. A. J. Bliss, ed., *Sir Launfal* (London, 1960), ll. 223–48; 883–9.
18. On the identification of Launfal's fairy mistress with Morgan le Fay, see Eithne M. O'Sharkey, 'The identity of the Fairy Mistress in Marie de France's Lai de Lanval,' *Bibliographical Bulletin of the International Arthurian Society*, vol. XXI (1969), 146–7.
19. A. J. Bliss, ed., *Sir Orfeo* (Oxford, 1954), ll. 279–306.
20. J. Huizinga, *The Waning of the Middle Ages* (Garden City, 1954), p. 54.
21. Sommer, Vol. V, *Le Livre de Lancelot del Lac* Part III, pp. 91–2.
22. Cf. Geoffrey of Monmouth's *Vita Merlini*, vv. 908–40.
23. On variant forms of her name see S. E. Holbrook, 'Nymue, the Chief Lady of the Lake, in Malory's Le Morte Darthur,' *Speculum*, vol. 53 (1978), 763.
24. Holbrook (p. 766) points out that Nymue's entire role here is Malory's addition.
25. Cf. *Sir Launfal*, ll. 1006–8 where Tryamour's breath blinds Guenevere.
26. See V. J. Harwood, *The Dwarfs of Arthurian Romance and Celtic Tradition* (Leiden, 1958).
27. See Raimond Van Marle, *Iconographie de L'Art Profane au Moyen-Age et à la Renaissance*, 2 vols. (New York, 1971), vol. 1, fig. 88, French tapestry, Musée des Gobelins; fig. 182, French tapestry, Musée de Cluny.
28. *Les Enchantemenz de Bretaigne An Extract from a Thirteenth Century Prose Romance, 'La Suite Du Merlin,'* ed. Patrick C. Smith (Chapel Hill, 1977) attempts to reproduce an accurate text based on the Cambridge Manuscript, Cambridge University Library Add. 7071, with the help of the Huth Manuscript, London, B.L. MS Add. 38117 and Paris, B.N. MS fr. 112. It is Malory's source for 'The Tale of King Arthur.' For the adventures of Gawain, Yvain, and Marhalt, see pp. 33–84.
29. Cf. the lays of *Graelent* and *Guingamor* and the fourteenth-century romance *Brun de la Montaigne*. See W. H. Schofield, 'The Lay of Guingamor,' *Harvard Studies and Notes in*

Philology and Literature, V (1896), 228–9; and Sara Sturm, *The Lay of Guingamor: A Study* (Chapel Hill, 1968), p. 30ff.

30. Patch, *The Otherworld*, pp. 144, 164, 195–216.
31. D. H. Green, 'The Pathway to Adventure,' *Viator*, vol. 8 (1977), 145–88.
32. E. R. Curtis in *European Literature and the Latin Middle Ages*, trans. W. R. Trask (New York and Evanston, 1963), p. 184, attributes Northern lions to epic stylization derived from the rhetorical school exercises of Late Antiquity.
33. On the tradition of the Wild Man-Knight, see R. W. Ackerman, 'Arthur's Wild Man Knight,' *RPH* 9 (1955), 115–19; Larry D. Benson, *Art and Tradition in Sir Gawain and the Green Knight* (New Brunswick, N.J., 1965); Richard Bernheimer, *Wild Men in the Middle Ages: A Study of Art, Sentiment, and Demonology* (Cambridge, Mass., 1952); Penelope B. R. Doob, *Nebuchadnezzar's Children; Conventions of Madness in Middle English Literature* (New Haven and London, 1974); Judith S. Neaman, *Suggestion of the Devil: The Origins of Madness* (Garden City, N.Y., 1975).
34. Doob, *op. cit.*, p. 134.
35. On the relationship of the hunt motif to chivalric adventure, and in particular the association between the white stag and an Otherworld lover, see M. B. Ogle, 'The Stag-Messenger Episode,' *American Journal of Philology*, vol. XXXVII.4, 387–416; Lucy A. Paton, *op. cit.*, pp. 228–247; K. G. T. Webster, *Guenevere, A Study of Her Abductions* (Milton, Mass., 1951), pp. 89–104.
36. Ogle, p. 402.
37. Paton, p. 229: 'In our study of fairy life we have by this time learned to suspect the vicinity of fairie when we find before our eyes a white stag and brachet, and a splendid uninhabited castle.'
38. Only Malory, his source the Old French prose *Tristan*, and the Italian *La Tavola Ritonda* give this version, a fact used by Ogle to substantiate the thesis that the 'Stag-messenger' episode has Classical rather than Celtic origins.
39. This allusion may be a remnant of the account in Geoffrey's *Historia* and Layamon's *Brut* where the Saxons, here confused with Saracens, are the chief enemies of the Britons.
40. See A. C. L. Brown, *Iwain, a Study in the Origins of Arthurian Romance*, 2nd ed. (New York, 1965), pp. 126ff.; C. B. Lewis, *Classical Mythology and Arthurian Romance* (Edinburgh, 1932), pp. 50ff.; J. K. Wright, *Geographical Lore of the Time of the Crusades* (New York, 1925), p. 50. T. P. Crosse's *Motif-Index of Early Irish Literature* (Bloomington, Indiana, 1939), D925, D926, and D927, associates fountains, wells, and springs with magic.
41. This is the reading in Cambridge University Library MS Add. 7071. The Huth *Merlin*, London, British Library MS Add. 38117 describes Merlin's appearance as that of 'un enfant de quatre ans' (Vinaver's note, p. 1298, 43.21), a reading that makes sense since a fourteen-year-old would look more like a man than a child. However, the illustrations in the Huth *Merlin* consistently depict the wizard as 'shorter than other characters and rather churlish in expression.' B.L. MS Add. 10292, f.200 shows Merlin disguised as a boy wearing a brown kirtle and plain (unpointed) shoes, and carrying a club.
42. See Patch, *The Otherworld*, pp. 251–6 and Paton, *op. cit.* pp. 15–18.
43. Northrop Frye, *Anatomy of Criticism* (New York, 1966), p. 183.

4: The Way to Corbenic

1. The text of Malory's source is available in H. O. Sommer, *The Vulgate Version of the Arthurian Romances* (Washington, 1913), vol. VI; Albert Pauphilet, ed., *La Queste del Saint Graal* (Paris, 1949); *The Quest of the Holy Grail*, trans. P. M. Matarasso (Harmondsworth, 1969).
2. On resemblances between the imagery of *La Queste* and the art of Reims cathedral, see my article 'Christian Iconography in The Quest of the Holy Grail,' *Mosaic* XII/2 (1979), 11–19.
3. Emile Mâle, *The Gothic Image*, trans. Dora Nussey (New York, Evanston, and London, 1958), p. 29, originally published as *L'art religieux du XIIIe siècle en France* (Paris, 1902).
4. A. O. Lovejoy, *The Great Chain of Being* (New York, 1965), p. 83.
5. Ibid., p. 82.
6. Vinaver, *Works*, p. 1582, n. 1027.30–2, attributes the sword image to Malory's mistranslation

of the French *ung vent* (a wind). In any case, it is an error that conforms to the Old Testament picture of 'the Lord, strong and mighty, the Lord mighty in battle.'

7. Cf. the bestiary tradition as represented by T. H. White's *The Bestiary, A Book of Beasts being a Translation from a Latin Bestiary of the Twelfth Century* (London & New York, 1954), pp. 132–3. Mâle, pp. 39–46, suggests that the bestiaries had little effect on art or on sermon literature until Honorius of Autun utilised such allegorical images as the pelican, the lion, the unicorn, the charadrius, and the dragon in his *Speculum Ecclesiae* (ca. 1090–1120). The pelican was one of the most popular decorative devices in medieval English churches. See *inter alia* M. D. Anderson, *Animal Carvings in British Churches* (Cambridge, 1938); C. J. P. Cave, *Roof Bosses on Medieval Churches* (Cambridge, 1948); J. C. Cox, *Bench Ends in English Churches* (Oxford, 1916); Arthur Gardner, *English Medieval Sculpture* (New York, 1973 [1935]); and G. L. Remnant, *Catalogue of Misericords in Great Britain* (Oxford, 1969). The most comprehensive reference on religious iconography is Louis Réau's *Iconographie de L'Art Chrétien* (Paris, 1955), 3. vols.

8. On the iconography of Christ and the four evangelists see Mâle, *op. cit.*, pp. 7, 35–7; and F. P. Pickering, *Literature and Art in the Middle Ages* (Coral Gables, Florida, 1970), pp. 127–9.

9. This theory of authorship suggested by Albert Pauphilet in *Etudes sur la Queste del Saint Graal*, (Paris, 1921) is generally accepted. On the monastic spirit of *La Queste* see also Jean Frappier, 'The Vulgate Cycle' in *ALMA*, p. 306. The theological background is elucidated by Etienne Gilson, 'La Grâce et Le Saint Graal' *Les Idées et Les Lettres* (Paris, 1955), pp. 59–91.

10. C. G. Jung, 'Transformation Symbolism in the Mass,' *Pagan and Christian Mysteries* (New York, 1963), p. 93.

11. Similarly, Adam, Noah, Abraham, David, Solomon and Melchizedek were regarded as types of Christ. In medieval cathedrals their statues formed a *via sacra* leading to Christ. Cf. Mâle, pp. 152–7, and Henri Foçillon, *The Art of the West in the Middle Ages*, vol. 2, *Gothic Art*, trans. Donald King, ed. Jean Bony (London and New York, 1963), p. 75.

12. Sommer, vol. VI, p. 28ff.

13. On Celtic sources and analogues cf. A. C. L. Brown, *The Origin of the Grail Legend* (Cambridge, Mass., 1943); R. S. Loomis, *Celtic Myth and Arthurian Romance* (New York, 1927); R. S. Loomis, *The Grail from Celtic Myth to Christian Symbol* (Cardiff and New York, 1963); Helaine Newstead, *Bran the Blessed in Arthurian Romance* (New York, 1939); H. R. Patch, *The Other World* (Cambridge, Mass., 1950).

14. The idea that between the Crucifixion and Resurrection, Christ journeyed to Hell to release the souls of the just from Satan's bond is found first in the fifth century *Gospel of Nicodemus*. See *The Apocryphal New Testament*, trans. M. R. James (Oxford, 1924); *The Middle-English Harrowing of Hell and the Gospel of Nicodemus*, ed. W. H. Hulme, EETS ES vols. 100, 101 (London, 1907).

    The *Saint Omer Hours*, ca. 1350, London, B. L. MS Add. 36684, fol. 60 shows a Harrowing of Hell where the souls emerge from the cave-like and fiery Hell's-mouth moving towards a white Christ holding the cross of the Resurrection while a black Devil looks on helplessly. The scene is not unlike that described in Malory, p. 1026; Galahad descends through a cave into a flaming tomb where he is haled as one who 'may draw oute the soules of erthely payne and (to) putte them into the joyes of Paradyse'.

    Another aspect of the Harrowing of Hell, the idea that Christ attacked the gates of Hell, may be represented in medieval literature and art as an attack on a demonic castle.

15. Cf. the crucifix (ca. 1200) in the Archbishop's Museum, Utrecht, depicting a noble and composed Christ wearing a crown to which the hand of God is pointing; an ivory book cover (first half of eleventh century), Eglise de Notre-Dame, Liège, reproduced in George Henderson, *Early Medieval* (Harmondsworth, 1977), fig. 149, where two angels hover bearing a crown above Christ's head; a twelfth century Spanish processional cross and a thirteenth century shrine from Limoges, both in the Metropolitan Museum of Art, New York.

16. On the medieval image of the Cross as a bed see F. W. Locke, *The Quest for the Holy Grail: A Literary Study of a Thirteen Century French Romance* (Stanford, 1960), p. 91.

17. Cf. T. H. White, *The Book of Beasts*, pp. 7–8. Like the pelican, the lion was a popular decorative device in church art. See above, note 7.

18. On the temporal and theological symbolism of Pentecost see F. W. Locke, pp. 40–64.

19. The centrality of the rose image in Dante is discussed by H. F. Dunbar, *Symbolism in Medieval Thought and Its Consummation in the Divine Comedy* (New York, 1961), pp. 3–4, 79–80.
20. The dove image in Christian art was particularly associated with the scene of Christ's baptism and with the Annunciation.
21. The formative influence on medieval angelology was the Celestial Hierarchies of Pseudo-Dionysius. See C. S. Lewis, *The Discarded Image* (Cambridge, 1967), pp. 70–5.
22. Cf. Dante, *Paradiso XXVIII*, 133–5.
23. Cf. also pp. 1012, 1014, 1015, 1027–8.
24. The motif of angels carrying souls to heaven, often in what looks like a table napkin, is common both in church art and manuscript illustration. The Angel Choir in Lincoln Cathedral provides some examples. Cf. also the *Lansdowne Psalter*, mid-twelfth century, London, B.L. MS Landsdowne 383 fol. 168ᵛ; Wolfram von Eschenbach, *Willehalm*, Vienna, Der Osterreichischen Nationalbibliothek, MS Codex Vindobonensis 2670, fol. 351. New York, Morgan Library MS M805, fol. 1 shows an angel carrying king Ban's soul.
25. Jean Frappier, 'Le Graal et La Chevalerie,' *Romania* LXXV (1954), pp. 165–210.
26. Paul Zumthor, *Merlin le Prophète* (Lausanne, 1943), pp. 128–9.
27. Etienne Gilson, in 'La Mystique de la Grâce dans la Queste del Saint Graal,' *Romania*, LI (1925), 321–37, suggests that St Bernard of Clairvaux was the probable source of the mystical doctrines in *La Queste*.
28. Rosemond Tuve, *Allegorical Imagery*, p. 342.
29. In the previously cited essay, Frappier attributed the Church's rejection of the Grail legends to the fact that they allowed to knights the possibility of attaining spiritual experiences. The *Catholic Encyclopaedia* grounds its rejection on the priority that the legends gave the Church of Britain over the Church of Rome. If the theory of Gnostic origins put forward by Leonardo Olschki's *The Grail Castle and its Mysteries*, trans. J. A. Scott (Manchester, 1966) is correct, heresy would have made the legends untenable. A result of the legends' failure to gain the Church's approval is that the manuscripts of the Grail romances have been preserved not in monasteries but in the libraries of the aristocracy.
30. Eugene Vinaver, *Malory* (Oxford, 1929), p. 77.
31. An iconographical device for representing Christ's lineage, the Tree of Jesse was adapted particularly to the medium of stained glass, as, for example, at St Denis, Chartres, Le Mans, Sainte-Chapelle. The oldest stained glass in England is a seated Jesse figure (ca. 1150) on the North Aisle window of York Minster. On the origins and development of the motif, see Elisabeth von Witzleben, *French Stained Glass* (London, 1968), pp. 23–5. It also appeared on the *Beatus* page of psalters.
32. On Perceval's sister as a type of the Virgin, see F. W. Locke, pp. 76–7 and Myrrha Lot-Borodine, *Trois Essais sur le Roman de Lancelot du Lac et La Quete du Saint Graal* (Paris, 1919), p. 54. Locke also discusses the significance of Perceval's aunt, p. 75. In 'Malory and the Grail Legend,' *Selected Writings*, ed. Anne Ridler (London, 1961), p. 160, Charles Williams sees the relationship between Perceval and his sister as 'not so much the significance of kinship in blood as of kinship in spirit . . . it is conjoined love, but love conjoined in the Grail'.
33. See White, *The Bestiary*, 165–7.
34. For the patristic sources of the symbolism, see Pauphilet, pp. 106ff.
35. *op. cit.*, p. 24.
36. Edgar de Bruyne, *Etudes d'Esthétique Médiévale* (Brugge, 1946), 3 vols., vol. III, pp. 9–29.
37. *op. cit.*, I, p. 304.
38. On medieval colour symbolism, see de Bruyne, I, p. 298 and Frederic de Portal, *Des Couleurs Symboliques dans l'Antiquité, le Moyen Age et Les Temps Modernes* (Paris, 1857).
39. 'De Administratione' in *Abbot Suger on the Abbey Church of St-Denis and its Art Treasures*, 2nd ed., ed. and trans. Erwin Panofsky (Princeton, 1979 [1946]), pp. 62–5 (Latin text included).
40. On Irish analogues of the threatening spear and Perilous Bed see R. S. Loomis, *The Grail from Celtic Myth to Christian Symbol*, pp. 49, 74–9, 153–5. A survey of scholarship dealing with the Celtic origins of the lance is found in Rose Peebles, *The Legend of Longinus* (Baltimore, 1911), pp. 166ff. On the lance of Longinus as a Christian symbol see Peebles, pp. 56ff. In the Vulgate Prose cycle the *Lance Vengeresse* is described as the lance that pierced Christ's side and that wounded Bors and Gawain in the adventure of the Perilous Bed. It is also the lance with which Balin delivered the Dolorous Stroke. Cf. Sommer II, 334–45; IV, 344–5; 298.

41. Cf. Réau, *Iconographie de L'Art Chrétien*, vol. II, pp. 60–3. A more sophisticated concept, paralleled by Perceval's demonic lady, is the representation of the devil as a handsome, worldly member of medieval society. A devil of this kind appears in Chaucer's 'Friar's Tale' and on the West front of Strasbourg Cathedral.

42. I do not accept Vinaver's view that Malory's Grail quest is just another Arthurian adventure and that 'his one desire seems to be to secularize the Grail theme as much as the story will allow' (1535). Some objections to Vinaver's ideas are expressed by C. S. Lewis in 'The English Prose Morte,' *Essays on Malory*, ed. J. A. W. Bennett (Oxford, 1963), pp. 14–20.

43. Tuve calls the pilgrimage of human life motif 'the basic allegorical theme'. See her analysis of Guillaume de Deguileville's 'Pèlerinage de la vie humaine' in *Allegorical Imagery*, pp. 145–218.

44. Locke, p. 59, cites a passage in Lactantius, *Divinae Institutiones*, P.L. 6, col. 797, where a sword signifies the Second Coming of Christ. Since Galahad is a type of Christ, the allusion is not irrelevant.

45. *John* 20, 19.

46. *Selected Writings*, p. 158.

47. ibidem, p. 159.

48. Pauphilet, p. 113.

49. Fernand Lot, *Etude sur le Lancelot en Prose* (Paris, 1954), p. 418.

50. Pauphilet, p. 54ff. Fernand Lot expresses reservations about Cistercian authorship of the *Lancelot*; see *Romania* XLIX (1923), 433–41. While Jean Frappier in *Étude Sur La Mort Le Roi Artu* (Paris, 1961), pp. 219ff. admits Cistercian influence, he notes a curious lack of theological disquisition in *La Mort*.

51. *Ephesians* 6, 11–17.

52. On the broken sword motif in French romance, see A. E. Waite, *The Holy Grail* (New York, 1961), pp. 70–3.

53. See Constance B. Hieatt, *The Realism of Dream Visions* (The Hague-Paris, 1967).

54. See Mâle, pp. 98–130; Tuve, pp. 57–143; A. E. M. Katzenellenbogen, *Allegories of the Virtues and Vices in Mediaeval Art from Early Christian Times to the Thirteenth Century* (London, 1939); Helen Woodruff, *The Illustrated Manuscripts of Prudentius* (Cambridge, Mass., 1930); and a reconstruction of the influential twelfth-century manuscript of Herrad of Hohenbourg's *Hortus Deliciarum*, 2 vols., ed. R. Green, M. Evans, C. Bischoff, and M. Curschmann (London and Leidon, 1979), vol. II, figs. 258–85.

55. On the Seven Deadly Sins as knights, see Morton Bloomfield, *The Seven Deadly Sins, an Introduction and a History of a Religious Concept with Special Reference to Medieval English Literature* (East Lansing, Mich., 1952).

56. Cf. fn. 14.

57. On the importance of dogma in *La Queste*, see L. A. Fisher, *The Mystic Vision in the Grail Legend and in the Divine Comedy* (New York, 1966); Etienne Gilson, 'La Grâce et le Saint-Graal'; F. W. Locke, *The Quest for the Holy Grail*, pp. 121, 227; Albert Pauphilet, *op. cit.*, pp. 27–84.

58. On the efficacy of intercession, abstinence, divine favour and faith in *La Queste*, see Pauphilet, pp. 27ff., 64ff.

59. Cf. 863, 28–31, 930, 14–18.

60. The lion's similarity to a canine pet might have been suggested by iconographical associations with St Mark, the evangelist whose symbol is a lion, and St John the Baptist whose life in the Wilderness is signified by an accompanying lion. The *Grandes Heures de Rohan*, ca. 1420, Paris, B.N. MS lat. 9471 fol. 23 shows St Mark patting the head of a spaniel-like lion that fawns upon him. The *Petites Heures of John, Duke of Berry*, ca. 1388, Paris, B.N. MS. lat. 18014 fol. 208 shows John the Baptist sitting at the entrance to a cave and stroking the mane of a lion that is supported on his lap.

61. On typological symbolism, see Réau, vol. 1, pp. 192–222. In 'The Allegory of Church and Synagogue,' *Speculum* XIV (1939), 448–64, Margaret Schlauch notes that there was a close connection between the literary motif of Church and Synagogue found in the French Arthurian romances *Perlesvaus* and *La Queste* and an important body of theological writings produced around 1200 AD. During the same period there were also numerous representations in art with Church generally represented as a crowned woman carrying a chalice while a

blindfolded Synagogue carries a broken standard or broken spear (an instrument of the Passion) as the Table of the Law falls from the other hand.

62. The Crucifixion was regarded as the point in history when Christ founded the Church and displaced the authority of the Synagogue; cf. cathedral windows at Bourges, Le Mans, Châlons-sur-Maine, Reims and Troyes. Other representations are sculptured figures like those at Strasbourg, Lincoln, and Rochester. The *Hortus Deliciarum* fig. 101 adds to the Crucifixion scene the association of Church and Synagogue with animals; the former rides a hybrid with four heads representing the evangelists, the latter is mounted on an ass. Even closer to the iconography of *La Queste* and Malory is the miniature in the *Hours of Yolande de Lalaing*, ca. 1450–60, Oxford, Bodleian MS Douce 93 fol. 100^v where the Crucifixion scene includes the crowned and haloed Church riding a lion. Interestingly, the border of this folio is ornamented with scenes from a tournament.

63. Locke, pp. 75–8.

64. Helen Hennessy, 'The Uniting of Romance and Allegory in La Queste du Saint Graal,' *Boston University Studies in English*, IV (1960), p. 193.

65. Wallace Stevens, *The Necessary Angel* (New York, 1951), p. 81.

66. Views of time and history will be discussed in Chapter 6.

67. See G. R. Owst, *Literature and Pulpit*, pp. 68–9 on the Ship of Faith as a popular homiletic figure.

68. The middle ages had evolved a complicated symbolism whereby the Tree of Life in the Garden of Eden provided the wood for the Tree of Death from which the Cross was made.

69. *Hortus Deliciarum* fol. 204^v (fig. 286 in 1979 edition) shows Solomon, crowned, reclining in an ornate bed which is identified with the Church: 'Lectulus Salemonis est celestis requies et presens Ecclesia in qua sancti amplexu veri pacifici delectantur, finita viciorum pugna' (vol. 2, p. 337).

70. R. S. Loomis suggests that the name is a corruption of *corbenoit* (blessed horn). See Helaine Newstead, *Bran the Blessed*, p. 89 and R. S. Loomis, *Wales and the Arthurian Legend* (Cardiff, 1956), pp. 41ff.

71. For Celtic analogues of the Perilous Bed and threatening lance see A. C. L. Brown, *The Origin of the Grail Legend*, p. 132ff.; R. S. Loomis, *Celtic Myth and Arthurian Romance*, p. 158ff.; Jean Marx, *La Légende Arthurienne et Le Graal* (Paris, 1952), pp. 117–39. The adventure of the Perilous Bed is associated with Gawain in the *Prose Lancelot*. His adventures in the Grail quest have been translated by J. L. Weston under the title *Sir Gawain at the Grail Castle* (London, 1903).

72. The arrival at night is a convention of Grail literature. See R. S. Loomis, *Celtic Myth and Arthurian Romance*, p. 171.

73. Marx, *op. cit.*, p. 140, points out that in Celtic myth the Otherworld castle was generally situated by the sea.

74. The lion was traditionally used as a sentinel at the door of sacred places.

75. In the French source, the lions lie down quietly. Malory's lions 'made sembelaunte to do hym harme'. Malory is perhaps trying to excuse Lancelot's drawing of the sword. A dwarf, not a flaming hand, knocks it away.

76. R. S. Loomis, *The Development of Arthurian Romance* (London, 1963), p. 106.

77. Olschki attributes the Grail's miraculous powers to its resplendent light which he interprets as a Gnostic symbol adopted by the Cathars, *op. cit.*, p. 20ff.

78. On the analogy between feasting in the hall of the Grail Castle and in the Otherworld castles of Irish myth see Jean Marx, p. 108ff. In both cases the castle is 'un monde ouvert' where a chosen hero can visit and receive entertainment before returning to the real world. Often the visit to the Otherworld castle is motivated by a desire to acquire some treasure.

79. On the Grail Procession in various texts see the Appendix to Jessie L. Weston's *The Quest of the Holy Grail*, 2nd ed. (London, 1964).

80. Etienne Gilson, 'La Grâce et le Saint Graal,' p. 61.

81. Jacques Maritain, *Art and Poetry* (New York, 1943), p. 47.

82. St Bernard, *De Gratio et libero arbitrio*, cap. VI, art. 18, in *Opera Omnia*, 3 vols., ed. J. Mabillon after J. P. Migne, *Patrologia latina* 182 (Paris, 1854), vol. 1, p. 1011.

5: The Colde Erthe

1. Elizabeth T. Pochoda in *Arthurian Propaganda, Le Morte Darthur as an Historical Ideal of Life* (Chapel Hill, 1971), pp. 130–40 argues that Arthur's inadequacy as king is the chief reason for his society's failure.
2. See R. M. Lumiansky, 'The Tale of Lancelot and Guenevere, Suspense' in *Malory's Originality, A Critical Study of Le Morte Darthur*, ed. R. M. Lumiansky (Baltimore, 1964), pp. 205–32 on the lovers' tempestuous relationship.
3. Joan Evans, *Dress in Mediaeval France* (Oxford, 1952), p. 42, and Huizinga, p. 120.
4. A. D. Hope, *A Midsummer Eve's Dream* (Canberra, 1970), p. 13.
5. See T. P. Cross and W. A. Nitze, *Lancelot and Guenevere* (Chicago, 1930) and K. G. T. Webster, *Guinevere: A Study of Her Abductions* (Milton, Mass., 1951).
6. J. D. Bruce ed. *Le Morte Arthur, A Romance in stanzas of eight lines re-edited from MS. Harley 2252 in the British Museum* E.E.T.S., No. 88 (London, 1959 [1903]). On Malory's use of this work in his last two books see R. H. Wilson, 'Malory, the Stanzaic Morte Arthur, and the Mort Artu, *Modern Philology* 37 (1939), 125–38; E. Talbot Donaldson, 'Malory and the Stanzaic Le Morte Arthur', *Studies in Philology*, 47 (1950), 460–72, and Vinaver, *Works*, pp. 1585–1663.
7. Ornamental chains became popular adornments in the late fourteenth century. They are depicted in the Jardin d'Amour, a picture painted for Jean sans Peur about 1415. See the reproductions, plates 46 and 47 in Joan Evans, *Dress in Mediaeval France* (Oxford, 1952).
8. Joan Evans, p. 60, citing Chastellain, *Chroniques*, Pt. I, ch. xvii.
9. See V. F. Hopper, *Medieval Number Symbolism* (New York, 1938).
10. Edgar de Bruyne, *Etudes d'esthétique médiévale*, II, 195.
11. J. Huizinga, *The Waning of the Middle Ages* (Garden City, 1954), pp. 28–9.
12. G. R. Stewart, 'English Geography in Malory's Morte D'Arthur,' *Modern Language Review*, 30 (1935), 204–9.
13. On Malory's likely participation in the Wars of the Roses, see Vinaver, *Works*, xxv; William Matthews, *The Ill-framed Knight: a Skeptical Inquiry into the Identity of Sir Thomas Malory* (Berkeley, 1966); Gweneth Whitteridge, 'The Identity of Sir Thomas Malory, Knight-Prisoner,' *Review of English Studies*, N.S. 24 (1973), 257–65; Richard R. Griffith, 'The Political Bias of Malory's Morte Darthur,' *Viator*, 5 (1974), 365–86.
14. Vinaver, *Works*, pp. 1640–2.
15. Vinaver, *Works*, p. 1649, note 1233. 6–8.
16. *op. cit.* p. 39.
17. Cf. *Works* 1166, 1168.26–1169.3, 1183.27–1184.11, 1201.9–22, 1230.18–1231.3.
18. See J. Huizinga, *The Waning of the Middle Ages*, ch. XIX, 'Art and Life,' pp. 242–64, and Otto Cartellieri, *The Court of Burgundy* (London, 1929). Feasting, maying, hawking and other courtly pastimes were frequently depicted in the calendars of fifteenth century Books of Hours. See particularly the facsimile editions of the Chantilly; Museé Condé MS, *Les Très Riches Heures du Duc de Berry* (London, 1969) and New York, The Metropolitan Museum of Art, The Cloisters Collection, *The Belles Heures of Jean, Duke of Berry, Prince of France* (New York, 1958).
19. Miguel de Unamuno, *The Tragic Sense of Life*, trans. J. E. C. Flitch (Macmillan, 1921), p. 21.

6: Patterns of Time

1. Cf. Eugène Vinaver, pp. 618, 620–1, 625–6, 633. The Saxons were the traditional enemies of the Britons both in the histories of Gildas, Nennius, Geoffrey of Monmouth *et al* and in such literary works as Wace's *Roman de Brut* and Layamon's *Brut*.
2. *op. cit.* xxxi–xxxii; 1396–7; 1649.
3. The linear view was given a universal chronology in the seventh century by Isidore of Seville who made the birth of Christ the central point of reference for historical events. Popularized by Bede in *De temporibus* and *Historia Ecclesiastica*, and transmitted by St Boniface to the continent this method of dating was adopted by the Vatican in 1048.
4. Cf. Asser's King Alfred, Suger's Saint Louis and Bede's Oswald.

5. See the analyses in Lord Arthur Raglan's *The Hero* (London, 1936).
6. See R. F. Brinkley, *Arthurian Legend in the Seventeenth Century* (Baltimore, 1932).
7. Thirteenth and fourteenth century illustrators of *La Queste del Saint Graal* emphasize the typology by reproducing the models used for the Fall, the slaying of Abel, and the Harrowing of Hell in psalters and bibles. Cf. London, British Library MS. Add. 10294 and Royal 14 E iii.
8. Bors visits Corbenic sometime within the twelve month period following Galahad's birth for he must joust with Bromell la Pleche who is keeping La Pounte Corbyn for that period. When Elaine complains that Lancelot has not been back since his first visit, Bors replies that he has been in Morgan's prison for half a year. Book III recounts his capture by the fees, who found him sleeping under an apple tree.
9. See R. M. Lumiansky, 'The Question of Unity in Malory's *Morte Darthur*,' Tulane University *Studies in English*, V (1955), 35–9; Charles Moorman, 'Internal Chronology in Malory's *Morte Darthur*,' *JEGP*, 60 (1961), 240–9; R. H. Wilson, 'Chronology in Malory' in E. Bagby Atwood and Archibald A. Hill, eds., *Studies in Language, Literature and Culture of the Middle Ages and Later* (Austin, Texas, 1969), pp. 324–34, and Ellyn Olefsky, 'Chronology, Factual Consistency, and the Problem of Unity in Malory,' *JEGP*, 68 (1969), 57–73.
10. Cf. *Works*, pp. 16, 120, 178–9, 286, 293, 296–7, 336, 475–6, 832, 839, 853, 1098, 1121, 1145.
11. The best known classification of the ages of man is that of the Greek poet Hesiod who, in *Works and Days*, portrayed the human race progressively declining from a Golden Race made by Chronos to the Silver Race of the Olympians, the Bronze Race of Zeus, the Homeric Race of heroic men and the Race of Iron, 'wretches who know not the visitations of the Gods.' Greek astronomers estimated that it took a thirty-six thousand year period (the Great Year) for one complete cycle from golden age to golden age. Medieval man could have read accounts of the golden age in Ovid's *Metamorphoses* I, ll. 89–112; Virgil's *Aeneid* VIII, ll. 313–28; Boethius' *Consolation of Philosophy*, II, poem 5.
12. William Caxton, Epilogue to 'The Order of Chivalry,' *The Prologues and Epilogues of William Caxton*, ed. W. J. B. Crotch, EETS, O.S. 176 (London, 1928).
13. V. A. Kolve, *The Play Called Corpus Christi* (Stanford, 1966), p. 102.
14. See Erich Auerbach's comparison of linear or horizontal time based on a sequence of causation with vertical time based on figural relationships, in *Scenes from the Drama of European Literature*, trans. Ralph Manheim (New York, 1959), p. 72.
15. See Etienne Gilson, 'La Grace et le Saint Graal', *Les Idées et les Lettres* (Paris, 1955).
16. *Anatomy of Criticism*, p. 210.
17. *The Theological Tractates and the Consolation of Philosophy*, ed. H. F. Stewart and E. K. Rand (London, 1918), p. 400.